GW00671047

THE FINE

ARTS

SERIES

THEORY AND PRACTICE

HOW TO USE OIL PAINTS:
BASIC TECHNIQUES

Acknowledgements

The Fine Arts Series was originated by
Pieter van Delft and
Bert Willem van der Hout,
Alpha Design, Amsterdam.

Design: Bert Willem van der Hout,
Alpha Design, Amsterdam

Cover photo: Pieter Paul Koster
With thanks to: Hanno Rol

Translation by: Carla van Splunteren
and Tony Burrett

Typesetting: Euroset BV, Amsterdam,
The Netherlands

Lithography: Nefli BV, Haarlem
The Netherlands

Printing: Royal Smeets Offset BV
Weert, The Netherlands

Illustrations:
(l=left, r=right, a=above, b=below)

Siert Koning, Amsterdam:
page 74.

Koninklijke Smeets Offset BV, Weert:
pages 10, 16 *r*, 17 *l*, 53 b, 54, 55, 56, 57, 58,
59, 61 *r*, 63, 64, 65, 71, 72, 73, 82, 83, 84, 85,
86, 87, 88, 96 *r*, 97, 99 *r*, 105, 106, 107, 108,
110.

Martin Smit, Apeldoorn:
pages 70 b, 87.

Theo Stevens, Amsterdam:
pages 9, 13, 15 *l*, 16 *l*, 17 *r*, 19, 20, 21, 22, 23,
25, 26 *r*, 27 *r*, 28 *r*, 29 *r* + b, 30, 31, 33, 34, 35,
36, 37, 38, 39, 40, 42, 43, 44, 45, 46, 47, 48,
49, 50, 51, 52, 53 a, 60, 61 *l*, 62, 67, 68, 69,
70 a, 75, 76, 77 *l*, 78, 79, 80, 81, 89, 90, 91,
92, 93, 94, 95, 96 *r*, 99 *l*, 100, 101, 102, 103,
104, 109, 111, 112, 113, 114, 115, 116.

Koninklijke Talens BV, Apeldoorn:
pages 11, 14, 15 *r*, 18, 26 *l*, 27 *l*, 28 *l*, 29 *l*, 32,
41.

Paul Versteeg, Amsterdam:
page 77 *r*.

The publishers would like to thank (for
advice and materials):
Koninklijke Talens BV, Apeldoorn.
The importer of Hardtmuth products in
The Netherlands.

ISBN 0 7153 9474 6

© 1987 Royal Smeets Offset b.v.
Alpha Design, Amsterdam.

English edition © 1989 by
David & Charles plc, Newton, Abbot, Devon

First published in Great Britain 1989
by David & Charles plc, Newton Abbot,
Devon.

No part of this book may be reproduced in
any form, by print, photoprint, microfilm or
any other means without written permission
from the publisher.

Part I.

British Library Cataloguing in Publication Data
How to use oil paints: Basic techniques. –
(The Fine art series)

Oil paintings. Techniques. Amateurs'
manuals
I. Series
751.45

THE FINE

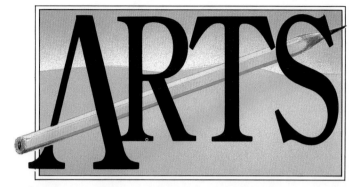

ARTS

SERIES

THEORY AND PRACTICE

HOW TO USE OIL PAINTS:
BASIC TECHNIQUES

DAVID & CHARLES
Newton Abbot · London

CONTENTS

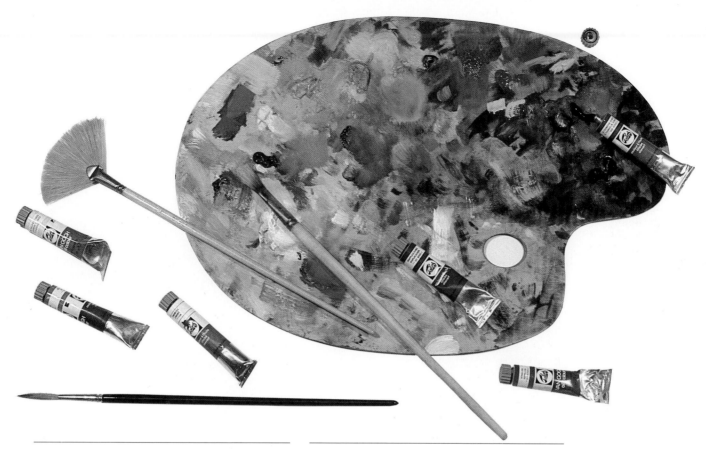

Portrait of a Man – 1433
JAN VAN EYCK

Was Jan van Eyck the true inventor of the medium of oil paint? It is certain that he searched for a long time for a method of binding pigments and colouring agents with linseed oil.

THE FINE ARTS SERIES

INTRODUCTION

Oil paint is a versatile material which, by the addition of the right amounts of oil, turpentine or painting medium, can be applied opaque or transparent, smooth or textured, matt or glossy.

The search for drying oils which could be incorporated into the paint was a lengthy process. Until well into the Middle Ages, tempera, an emulsion paint based on egg yolks and albumen, was the prevalent type of paint, and originally oil was added to it.

The discovery of oil paint is often ascribed to the Flemish painter Jan van Eyck (1390-1441), but this has never been proved for certain. He was, in any event, the first of the great masters to paint in oils.

In 1420, after many experiments, Van Eyck, by adding linseed oil, walnut oil and turpentine, produced a type of paint which was water resistant and which appeared to have good binding and drying properties. Since then, oil paint has undergone rapid development and not long after 1420 it became the normal painting material.

Before the 18th century, when the first ready-made oil paints, packed in pigs' bladders, became commercially available, an artist had to grind his own paints and prepare his own painting mediums.

This preparation took a great deal of time, but also provided the artist with an opportunity for building up a broad technical knowledge of his materials.

In addition, the intensity of the preparation ensured that no more of a material was produced than was necessary.

Nowadays, of course, things are rather different.

After the manufacture of oil paints got into its stride during the 19th century, it was not long before every conceivable painting material became available.

In fact, the assortment is now so wide that there is a chance of confusion. One of the intentions of this first of two volumes on oil painting is to familiarize you, step by step, with the assortment, beginning with the basic materials. This will be covered in more detail in the second volume.

Before the invention of metal tubes, painters ground their own oil paints. The pigments were stored in pigs' bladders. Those in the illustration were once owned by Rembrandt.

BASIC MATERIALS:
THE FIRST PURCHASES

SELECTION OF OIL PAINTS

There is a very wide assortment of oil paints available. Indeed, there are manufacturers who produce more than 120 colours!

In addition to professional oils, there are also students' paints which are primarily intended for the beginner. The difference in quality is largely determined by the pigments these paints contain, and the concentration and purity of that pigment.

Expensive pigments such as cadmium and cobalt are almost never incorporated in students' paints, but are replaced by substitutes. This is sometimes stated on the tube of the colour concerned.

Students' and professional oil paints usually work well together, certainly if paints of the same brand are used. It is therefore possible to begin with students' paints and gradually switch over to professional paints.

Because of the great variety of paints on offer, it is not easy for a beginner to choose a basic assortment. Usually the tendency is to purchase too many tubes at the same time. This is not a good idea.

First, many of the colours you have purchased will not be used immediately, or may not be used at all and lie around for years. This will result in 'sweating': the oil separates out and oozes from the tube. Secondly, if too large a basic assortment is purchased, it is too easy to use ready-made shades and the constant use of the same kind of colours makes a painting dull.

The beginner, therefore, does well to learn to obtain the shades of colour he wants through mixing. It is also useful to have to experiment with mixing: the more you practise mixing, the easier it will become to create a particular required colour. During mixing, it will also be discovered at what point the colour remains bright or, conversely, becomes 'dirty'. To this can be added that after a few years every painter develops his own palette, a palette that is attuned to his personal preference.

As a guide, we indicate how a basic assortment can be selected, but it should be borne in mind that this is only a suggested assortment. It has been selected so that by means of mixing the various colours, a broad colour spectrum can be attained.

WHITE   **Zinc white**

Zinc white results from the process of oxidation of zinc. Because of its purity it gives clear, bright shades when mixed with other colours.

YELLOW   **Cadmium lemon**

Cadmium is derived from cadmium ore. It is an expensive pigment. Depending on the method of preparation, cadmium can vary from cadmium lemon, light and dark yellow to orange, and vivid and deep red. In students' paints this expensive pigment is usually replaced by substitutes.

Cadmium yellow – deep
(see cadmium lemon)
Cadmium red – light
(see cadmium lemon)

RED   **Madder lake – deep**

Madder lake is obtained from the root of the madder plant. Depending on the method of preparation, madder lake is light or dark in colour. Nowadays, madder lake is made of a manufactured pigment called Alizarine, which has a similar composition to madder lake.

BLUE   Cobalt blue – light

Cobalt blue is made from cobalt sulphate. It is an expensive pigment which is replaced by substitutes in students' paints. There is a distinction between light and deep cobalt blue and cobalt violet.

Cerulean blue

Cerulean blue is also made from cobalt sulphate. It is a little greener than cobalt blue.

Ultramarine – deep

Ultramarine was once prepared from very finely ground lapis lazuli – a semi-precious stone. Once very costly it is now manufactured synthetically and has become one of the cheapest pigments. Colours are ultramarine light and deep, ultramarine red and ultramarine violet.

BROWN   Yellow ochre

Ochre is one of the oldest 'earth' pigments and derives its colour from iron oxide. Nowadays, ochre is made synthetically which means the colour is always the same, in contrast to the constantly differing colours derived from the original earth.

Burnt sienna

Sienna is related to the ochres. It is a yellow pigment which obtains its reddish-brown colour through burning. The name derives from *Terra di Sienna* – Sienna earth.

Burnt umber

Like ochre and sienna, umber is a mineral pigment. It contains a high proportion of manganese compounds. The deep brown colour is the result of burning. The name derives from *Terra di Umbria* – Umbria earth. Colours are greenish to deep brown.

BLACK   Ivory black

Ivory black was made by carbonising pure ivory. Nowadays, this black has been replaced by other carbonised animal products.

The basic assortment contains 12 tubes – 10 colours and black and white. The latter are not regarded as colours because they do not contain colours of the spectrum.

BRUSHES

There is perhaps an even greater assortment of brushes available than colours of oil paint. These differ from each other not only in shape but also in type of hair used.

There are short- and long-haired brushes, round and flat, blunt and pointed, wide and narrow, thick and thin, soft and stiff, fan-shaped and oval brushes.

The types of hair used include, among others, hog's hair, ox hair, squirrel hair and red sable hair. Besides these, there is also artificial hair, the so-called 'filament', which is a good alternative for the soft, expensive red sable hair.

Brushes have a number which indicates the thickness of the bundle of hairs it contains. Some series are numbered from 00 to 12, in other series only even numbers, 2 to 24, are used. The lower the number, the smaller the bundle of hairs. The higher the number, the larger, and therefore thicker, the bundles are. The thickness of brushes of the same number can differ from manufacturer to manufacturer. Obviously, the thickness of a brush determines its price: the thicker, the more expensive. A brush which is much thinner than can be expected from a particular number should not be purchased – that would be throwing money away.

The brush hairs are mounted in a metal sleeve (ferrule). In cheaper brushes this sleeve is nipped. The disadvantage of this is that during use the hairs tend to spread. The sleeve then weakens and the brush loses its hairs. Cheap then turns out to be expensive! Soldered sleeves, or better still, seamless sleeves are therefore more practical.

In this first volume we shall limit ourselves to the use of hog's hair and ox hair brushes of three types: the *Gussow*, a flat, short-haired (straight-cut) brush, and the round and flat (straight-cut) long-haired *Lyons brushes.*

Hog's hair is stiff and thick, each hair ending in two or more points. The best sort of hog's hair for these brushes is bleached Chinese hog's hair (Chunking). Stiff-haired brushes are particularly suitable for working with paste-like paint as the brush strokes remain visible.

Ox hair is soft and supple, the hairs tapering to a point. The tips of the hairs which come from the ears of the cow (this is cut and regrows) are lighter in colour. Brushes with soft hair are extremely suitable for working with thinned oil paint: the brush strokes tend to run, depending on the degree to which the paint is thinned. Which brush is chosen for painting in oils depends on a number of different factors.

Whether you wish to work to a large or a small format determines the width or thickness of the brushes you buy.

For working on large-format surfaces several thicker brushes and one thinner brush must be purchased.

Conversely, working to a smaller format requires more thin brushes and only one large brush.

As will already be apparent from the foregoing, stiff and soft brushes have different influences on the paint. In this volume both will be discussed and both types are included in the suggested list of brushes below. The idea is that you choose to buy between six and nine brushes from the list. Which brushes you buy depends on your own preference, but try to make your selection as varied as possible – thick and thin, short- and long-haired, flat and round, stiff- and soft-haired.

The brushes mentioned are good and not expensive.

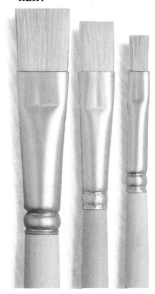

Fine-pointed, round brushes. Filament, manufactured from synthetic material, is a good alternative to the more expensive types of hair.

These Gussows are brushes with flat sleeves and short, straight-cut hair. They have long handles. The Gussows illustrated are of hog's hair.

Purchases according to your preference:

HOG'S HAIR: stiff	– short-haired, flat no. 6 – 10 – 18
	– Gussow long-haired, flat no. 6 – 10 – 18 Lyons brush
	– long-haired, round no. 6 – 10 – 18 Lyons brush

OX HAIR: soft	– short-haired, flat no. 6 – 10 – 18
	– Gussow long-haired, flat no. 6 – 10 – 18 Lyons brush
	– long-haired, round no. 6 – 10 – 18 Lyons brush

PALETTE KNIVES

Mixing certain quantities of oil paint with a brush has a number of disadvantages. First, it can result in air bubbles in the paint. Secondly, brushes, particularly soft-haired brushes, can lose their shape when used in this way. The hairs spread, the brush becomes deformed and can no longer be used effectively.

Palette knives are therefore used on the palette to mix larger amounts of paint with a medium or to mix colours together. Palette knives are stiff, straight metal knives and are available in various sizes. They are also used to collect paint which has spread over the palette and to scrape surplus paint off the palette.

A palette knife should never be used to apply paint to, or scrape paint off, the canvas, as this can damage it. This is partly due to the straight shape of the knife. The purchase of two palette knives – one small and one large, for example, is sufficient.

These Lyons brushes have flat sleeves and short, straight-cut hair. They have long handles. The brushes illustrated are of ox hair.

Palette knives are stiff, straight metal knives which must be used exclusively for working the paint on the palette.

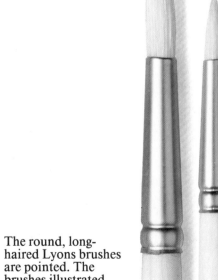

The round, long-haired Lyons brushes are pointed. The brushes illustrated are of hog's hair.

*Madonna With Child
and Two Angels
– c. 1460
FILIPPO LIPPI
Tempera on a panel.*

Until well into the
Middle Ages, artists
painted on wooden
panels, first with tem-
pera, a water-resistant
egg emulsion, later
with oil paint.

PAINTING KNIVES

In contrast to the stiff, straight palette
knife, painting knives are curved between handle and blade and are flexible.
They are made from thin, springy steel
and are used for various purposes.

Firstly, to transfer a larger quantity
of paint from the palette to the canvas
than would be possible with a brush.
Secondly, to transfer paint directly from
the tube to the canvas. Thirdly, to scrape
the paint on the canvas in order to
achieve particular effects, or to scrape
less successful layers of paint off the canvas. Fourthly, to replace or to complement the brushes, as is customary when
using the so-called knife technique. A
painting knife should never be used as
a palette knife, as the flexible metal can
bend or even break. The purchase of two
painting knives – one round and one
pointed – is sufficient for the moment.
If eventually you wish to develop your

Painting knives are
flexible metal knives,
which are curved
between the handle
and blade. They are
used exclusively for
transferring paint
from the palette to
the surface and for
working the paint on
the surface.

knife technique, you can always extend
your range of painting knives to include
those models which you consider to be
necessary.

SURFACES (SUPPORTS)

When oil paint is mentioned, one immediately thinks of canvas, but for a long
time wooden panels served as painting
surfaces (supports).

Canvas only came into use in the 15th
century. In the Middle Ages, the artists'
guilds exercised strict control over the
use of wooden panels. These had to be
free of knots and woodworm. With large,
important commissions, a thorough inspection of the panels was carried out
before painting commenced. If the stipu-
lated rules were breached, the artist was
immediately fined.

Nowadays, really good wooden panels
can rarely be obtained. If you are lucky,
you can perhaps lay your hands on good
small panels, and these usually come

OIL PAINTING PAPER AND HARD SURFACES

Paper without a prepared layer is unsuitable for painting in oils. The oil and the medium used for thinning the paint soak into the paper so that dull patches appear and the paint does not bind properly to the surface. The pigment particles lie on the surface, as it were, and therefore the paint and paper do not form a whole.

Oil painting paper is paper which is specially prepared for this type of paint. It is available in sheets of various sizes, 50 x 65 cm among others, from small to large. (50 x 65 cm is a universal format.)

Sometimes paper which is a multiple size of this format is offered and intermediate sizes also exist. This varies from manufacturer to manufacturer. Your supplier will furnish you with any information you require. Don't hesitate to ask!

You can also prepare heavy-quality drawing paper yourself by covering it on

Flute Player and Drummer – 1505
ALBRECHT DÜRER
Oils on a panel.

In the Middle Ages, wooden panels had to be of the highest quality. They were not allowed to contain knots and they had to be free of wood-worm.

Oil painting pads of various types. These vary in tint as well as in texture. The impregnated paper can be from pressed linen, but can also consist of impregnated cotton.

from old oak cabinets, oak being a commonly-used wood in those days. (Other sorts of wood used included walnut, linden and poplar.)

Old wood which comes from pieces of furniture will have been treated with oil, wax or varnish. Before the wood is suitable for painting, it must be leached, sandpapered and filled.

Unseasoned wood is unsuitable for painting in oils. It still contains too much sap and resin and this causes the wood to work. Cracks appear and the paint can blister. The canvas which is used everywhere nowadays is expensive and therefore a number of materials are being produced which can be used as an alternative, particularly for study purposes.

Oil painting paper and canvas board, for example, are perfectly satisfactory for making studies. Also, by covering and impregnating hard surfaces such as hardboard and chipboard yourself, you make experiments and studies affordable.

Hog's hair spalters
are eminently suitable
for impregnating sur-
faces.

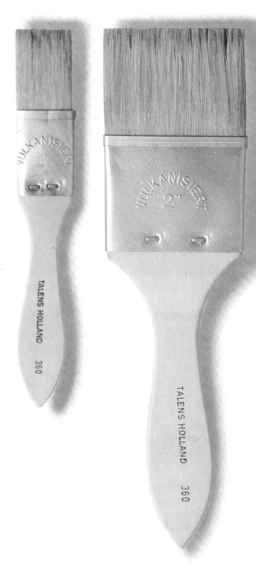

both sides with a thin layer of retouching
varnish. Retouching varnish is made
from colourless resins. A primer (Talens'
Gesso, for example) is also suitable for
this purpose. Coating the paper on both
sides helps to prevent it from rippling.
It is important to apply the varnish thinly
and to repeat the process.

For this impregnation, a broad, flat
brush, a *spalter*, is used. The width of a
spalter is always given in inches (1 in =
2.54 cm). Hog's hair spalters are the most
suitable for this purpose.

If you use retouching varnish, clean
your spalter in white spirit; if you use
Gesso, water should be used for cleaning.

CANVAS BOARD   Canvas board is stout
cardboard covered with canvas (cotton)
prepared with a coat of multi-purpose
finish.

It is prepared on one side only and
therefore the large sizes tend to warp
quickly. This can be prevented to some
extent by applying a coat of primer to the
back of the card. Oil painting card is
quite useful for trying out materials. If
the card still warps, even after the back
has been impregnated, then it can be cut
into smaller pieces before you begin your
experiments.

UNIVERSAL BOARD   Universal board is
board which is covered – with prepared
card – on the side intended for painting.
The back is covered in paper so that the
board does not deform. This board is
very suitable for making studies and it
keeps reasonably well. It absorbs mois-
ture easily, however, and is therefore
susceptible to changes in temperature.
This material should therefore be stored
in a dry place.

HARDBOARD   Hardboard is made of
pressed wood fibres. It is available in
sheets which can be cut in various sizes.
The width of the sheet is determined by
the capacity of the machines on which
they are produced. (The standard Euro-
pean size is 122 cm.)

Hardboard is quite suitable as a hard surface, as long as the format is not too large. Hardboard of a larger format than ± 50 x 65 cm can warp if it is not supported by a wooden frame.

Oil paint applied directly to a hardboard surface can be rejected, or conversely, so well absorbed that it almost disappears. In the latter event, it is the oil which is absorbed. In both cases the paint does not bind well with the surface and this means that the surface must first be prepared.

For this purpose a good primer is used. In earlier times, artists made their primers themselves and they developed many methods of preparation. Nowadays, ready-made primers are available, with oil as well as synthetic resin bases. An oil-based primer is suitable for priming a surface on which only oil paint will be applied. A primer based on synthetic dispersion is suitable for surfaces on which both oil paint and acrylic paint will be applied. The primer based on synthetic dispersion is also used for materials such as tempera, gouache and oil pastels. Because of its greater flexibility, we will use this primer for preparing undersurfaces for various painting and drawing materials. One well-known make is *Gesso*, manufactured by Talens.

IMPREGNATING A HARD SURFACE   Wash down the surface with white spirit to get rid of any possible greasy deposits. Use a spalter to impregnate the surface. Thin down a little Gesso in a bowl so that it is fluid enough to brush on easily. Sandpaper the smooth side of the hardboard. This allows the primer to be better absorbed. If you prefer to use the coarser back of the board – for a rougher painting technique in which the structure of the board is incorporated into the painting, for example – then sandpapering is not necessary.

Apply the first layer of Gesso. Sandpaper this layer into the surface while it is still wet. This gives a good bond

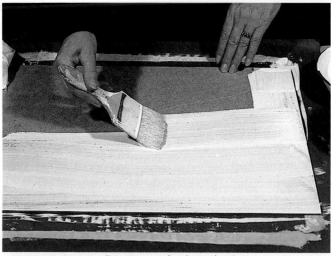

I Applying the first layer of primer in the impregnation of a surface.

II Sandpapering the still-wet layer.

between the primer and the surface. When this layer is thoroughly dry, apply a second layer. If the first layer was applied horizontally, apply the second crosswise – vertically – so that an optimum bond is obtained.

To prevent warping, a layer of primer should also be applied to the back of the board. Because this rough side absorbs a great deal of primer, it is more economical to use paperhanger's paste, a starch paste or a thinned water-based synthetic paste. Flexible glues (photographer's

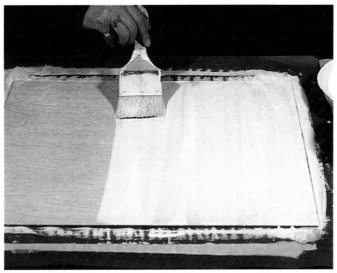

III   Applying the second layer of primer at right angles to the first.

can affect the plywood and cause the glue to loosen. The glue can also perish, resulting in the splitting of the layers. In addition, the glue can contain certain acids which affect the paint layer. Waterproof plywood, however, does not have these disadvantages.

COVERING A HARD SURFACE   For those who require more structure in the surface to be painted, it is possible to cover it with cotton or linen. This results in a surface which is very like canvas. You can use a piece of cotton, linen or cotton-linen mixture for this purpose. Synthetic fibres can also be used for covering surfaces. (Synthetic fibres are not a good alternative to canvas if they have to be mounted on a canvas stretcher because they tend to hang loosely.)

New material often contains *âpret* (starch) which can resist the absorption of oil paint. The cloth should therefore be first washed in a pure soap solution and then well rinsed in lukewarm water to remove all traces of soap. It should then be stretched out and allowed to dry. Unless it is absolutely necessary, the cloth should not be ironed, because this causes the fibres of the material to close. Open, they absorb the primer better.

Stiff cardboard, hardboard, fibreboard or chipboard can be used for covering with a cloth surface. Cut the material to size. Add 3 cm for the hem or for fixing to the edges.

We will use our primer – an excellent binding agent – as a glueing agent. The advantage of the composition of the glue and the primer being the same is that no unforeseen reactions between the materials – which could affect the surface – can take place.

Thin the primer with water until it is only just fluid enough to brush on easily. Roughen the surface a little with sandpaper so that the primer can better penetrate the fibres. Lay the cloth, the side to be used downwards, on a level surface

glue), are not suitable because they do not prevent warping.

When it is dry, the surface is ready to be used.

CHIPBOARD AND FIBREBOARD   Chipboard and fibreboard can both be used as hard surfaces. However, like hardboard, they must be impregnated before they are suitable for painting in oils. Bear in mind that in a large format these materials are rather heavy, and if such a large format is required, use a type which is not too thick. The method of preparation is the same as for hardboard. This type of surface should be handled with care. Because it consists of pressed fibres, the corners can easily be damaged by rough handling.

Wood materials, such as plywood, are also used as hard surfaces. There is no objection to using these for study purposes, as long as they are well prepared. We must, however, advise against the use of this type of material for making pieces of work which must stand the test of time. Plywood is comprised of layers of wood pressed together. Since it is not possible to determine the sort of glue used, one can never be sure about what will happen over a period of time. Damp

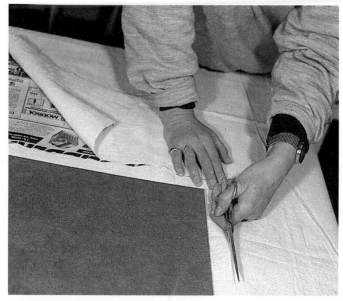

I The material is cut to size for mounting on the surface.

II A thick layer of primer is brushed onto the surface, which is then laid on the material.

III The corners must be cut obliquely.

IV The edges are folded over and pressed down firmly.

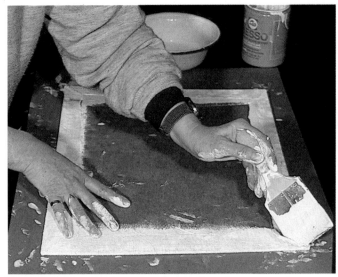

V A little extra primer can be used at the corners to ensure that the material binds properly.

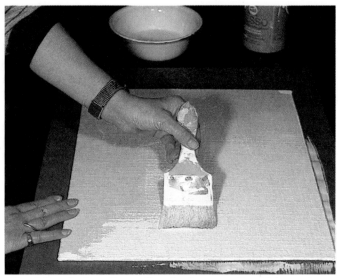

VI After drying, the surface is given another thin coat of primer, as an additional impregnated layer.

VII Paper is pasted on the surface's back to prevent warping.

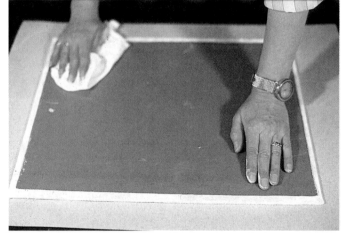

VIII Press the paper down firmly with a cloth to ensure that it binds properly.

IX Apart from white, a tinted ground is a good base for a painting.

covered with a clean sheet of paper. Use a spalter to brush a fairly thick layer of primer on the board and then lay this on the cloth, the layer of primer downwards. Turn the board over and brush the material smooth to that there are no creases.

Turn the board face downwards again and cut the corners of the material diagonally. Allow a surplus of approximately twice the thickness of the board. Fold over one long and one short side and carefully fasten down the corner. Repeat this for the other corners. Sometimes it is necessary to apply a little more primer. Allow the surface to dry and then apply a layer of thinned primer to the material.

Any warping of the surface can be removed by covering the back with paper that has been saturated with primer, or with paperhanger's paste or starch paste.

Cut the paper a little smaller than the surface format. Thin the primer or paste. It should have a watery consistency. Brush it on the paper and allow it to soak in. This removes the 'stretch' the paste has produced in the paper. Give the paper another coat of primer or paste. Lay it on the board and press it down firmly with a cloth.

Some painters prefer a tinted ground so that, by not covering it completely, they can allow it to play a part in the final painting. If you use a primer which contains oil, mix a little oil paint into it. With a synthetic-based primer, a little acrylic paint should be added to obtain a tint. Mixing a little paint into the primer produces a pastel shade; the colour you use will depend on the subject of your painting.

MOUNTING OIL PAINTING PAPER   Oil painting paper can also be mounted on a hard surface. This can be done before or after painting, but in the latter event the work must have an adequate layer of paint and there must be no porous areas. The painting must be thoroughly dry. Use a hard surface of the same format as the oil painting paper. Material

I

II

which can warp must be first impregnated on both sides. The impregnation of the upper side is necessary to prevent the paste or primer being absorbed, thus ensuring that the oil painting binds properly. The mounting can be carried out with paperhanger's paste, starch paste, synthetic resin glue or primer. Apply a substantial layer of paste or primer, using a spalter. It must not be thinned too much but should be just fluid enough to brush on easily.

Then lay the oil painting paper carefully on the surface. Cover it with a sheet of clean paper and brush it smooth. Lay it down flat, perhaps under a board. This applies a little pressure and assists the binding process.

If you do this after mounting a finished painting, do it carefully and make sure that it does not lie too long under pressure, in order to prevent damage to the paint layer.

I   For mounting oil painting paper, the surface is given a thick layer of primer. The painted or unpainted paper is then laid on the surface.

II   Care is necessary when pressing down the paper in order to prevent damage to the painting.

PALETTES

A palette serves to hold and mix the paint needed for the making of a painting. An oil paint palette is always flat. (A water paint palette contains small cups for the paint, because water paint is more fluid in consistency than oil paint and can therefore run.)

There are palettes for both left-handed and right-handed people. Remember when purchasing a palette that a right-hander holds the palette in his left hand and a left-hander holds it in his right. A left- or right-handed palette can be recognised by the position of the hole which fits the hollow between your thumb and forefinger. This serves to protect your hand.

Good wooden palettes are usually oiled, but many available palettes are varnished or completely untreated. Untreated wooden palettes must be treated with linseed oil, otherwise the oil from the paint will be absorbed by the wood. It is better to sandpaper and oil varnish palettes as soon as you buy them, because sooner or later the varnish layer will be damaged, causing the oil from the paint to be absorbed by the wood.

A wooden palette must be made from a short-fibred wood. The paint cannot penetrate wood of this sort and the palette will not splinter when you scrape off remnants of old paint.

Palettes are available in different shapes. When purchasing, make sure the palette lies comfortably in the hand, because while painting there is nothing more distracting than a palette which is uncomfortable to hold. The palette should be neither too small nor too big. A palette which is too small offers too little scope for mixing colours, while a palette which is too big is too heavy.

Try a number of palettes before buying. Push your thumb through the hole and bend your fingers in the hollow cut in the edge. Do not hold the palette away from you, but let it rest on your forearm.

Wooden palettes are used both inside and outside. For those who work inside and have plenty of space at their disposal, it is possible to use a small wheeled table as a palette. This must be covered, of course, with something that does not absorb oil from the paint. This surface must also be very smooth so that it will not be damaged when you scrape off remnants of old paint. A thick sheet of glass – milk glass is ideal – or a piece of white plexiglass are suitable for the purpose. You can also paint the undersurface of the glass (or the table surface) white. Do not use a tinted material, as this will influence your colours.

Particularly for painting outdoors, the so-called 'strip-off palettes' are extremely practical. They consist of prepared paper sheets assembled in a palette-shaped pad and this pad is handled in the same way as a palette. After the sitting (a working period is known as a sitting), the used sheet can be discarded. Not all painters are in favour of the strip-off palette. Especially if several sittings are necessary to complete a piece of work, a used palette can give an indication of the composition of the colour shades that have been created before. The used palette then functions as a sort of notebook and that can help a painter, especially a beginner, to remix a particular colour shade.

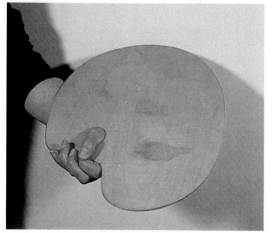

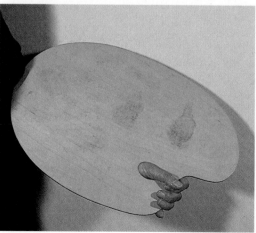

Oil painting palettes are available in various shapes and sizes. They are always completely flat.

Do not hold the palette away from you . . .

but support it on your forearm.

A good table easel can be folded up and because of this it does not take up much space when stored.

You can work on a table with this easel. A table easel can be used for surfaces of up to ± 60 cm.

EASELS

When painting in oils, the working surface is usually placed on an easel. Although small working surfaces can sometimes be laid on a table, the necessity of having an easel will soon become apparent.

Surfaces can be set on an easel in different ways: leaning forwards or backwards, or standing straight up. The height is also adjustable, so that you can work sitting or standing. You have a better overall view of a piece of work set on an easel, and paint and brushes can be handled more freely.

The purchase of an easel is an important business. The commonest types are table, studio and field easels. Your choice will firstly depend on your goal – are you going to work inside, outside, or both?

If you are going to work inside, what is the available space? Do you have to paint in the living room or do you have studio space? Is the space large or very small? These are all factors which will determine your choice. You must con-

sider carefully what is the most suitable easel for you personally.

The cost must also be considered, of course. Studio easels, particularly, are available in many different designs and at many different prices.

In any event, bear the following points in mind when making your purchase. Good wooden easels are made of beech (among other woods) which has been steamed or oiled. Check that the canvas-holder and the height regulator have been well designed and are strong enough, because they are often an easel's weakest features. A table easel must not be too small, because a small easel is not stable enough. A field easel must have a reliable telescopic system so that it can be easily set up and folded away again. Heavier studio easels must be mobile.

If you do not have much space, then choose a table easel so that you can work on a table. These are suitable for working surfaces of ± 60 cm. The easel must not be too small and it must fold away. Non-folding table easels are also available,

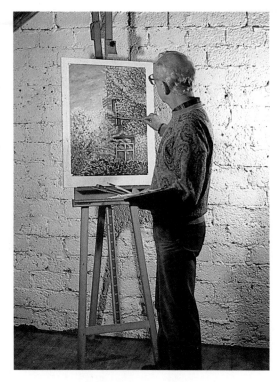

The folding three-legged easel is useful for the studio.

You can work sitting as well as standing at this easel. It can be used for surfaces of up to ± 135 cm.

but this is not a practical purchase if you have to make the most of the space at your disposal. A folding table easel can always be stored in some odd corner, or even hung on the wall. The table easel should also have a mechanism for adjusting the angle of the canvas.

The three-legged easel, suitable for working surfaces of up to ± 135 cm, is a useful studio easel which does not take up too much space because it can be stored flat against the wall. The height is adjustable so that you can work sitting or standing. The angle of inclination of the working surface can also be adjusted.

As we have already stated, large studio easels are available in various designs, from simple – and therefore cheaper – to very expensive models which have an electric mechanism for adjusting the

position of the canvas. A simple, solid studio easel, however, is sufficient for your requirements. You should have plenty of space at your disposal, for these easels are for studio use and stay in the same place when you are not working. They are also equipped with mechanisms to adjust the height and the angle of inclination of the working surface. These heavier types of easel are suitable for working surfaces of between approximately 120 and 235 cm. They also have wheels so that they are mobile.

When purchasing a studio easel, you should bear in mind the height of your ceiling. If you work on a large canvas, in a standing position, the arm holding the working surface will be quite high.

The field easel is intended for working 'in the field' but it can also be used inside as long as the working surface is not too large. These easels are not stable enough for large surfaces because the legs slip easily. Nevertheless, you can still work with a fairly large surface (up to approximately 100 cm) on a good field easel.

A studio easel must be stable. Obtain as much information as possible before purchasing.

A similar easel needs adequate working space. Depending on your requirements, it can be used to carry large surfaces of ± 120-235 cm.

Manufacturers strive to make these easels as light as possible without weakening their structure. On average they weigh between 1½ and 2 kilograms.

In practice, however, you will not work outside with oil paints very often. Factors such as transport, wind and rain must be considered. Moreover, a large surface involves a great deal of time and trouble; you will have to transport it often which increases the chance of damaging it. The field easel is not suitable for all painting techniques because its stability is not great enough for some of them. Knife techniques and making impastos, for example, require a firm easel because fairly heavy pressure is applied to the canvas. The stability can be increased by pushing the points at the ends of the

legs firmly into the ground, but this is not possible, naturally, if the easel is standing on a hard surface.

(Field easels are also suitable for water colour painting because they can be set horizontally, a position which is usually best for this technique.)

From the above, it is apparent that all the advantages and disadvantages must be carefully considered before an easel is purchased. If you do not want to purchase one immediately, a chair can be used as a temporary alternative. Place the canvas on the seat, leaning against the chair back, and sit on a stool in front of it.

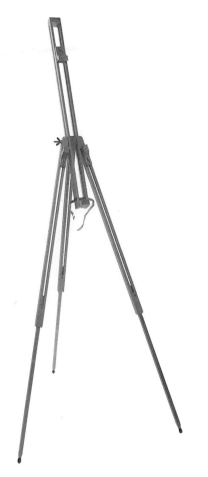

A field easel is collapsible for ease of transportation and should not weigh more than 1½ to 2 kg. This easel is intended for working outdoors, but it can also be used indoors. However, this easel is not stable enough for large working surfaces.

If you do not own an easel, an old kitchen chair can be used as an alternative.

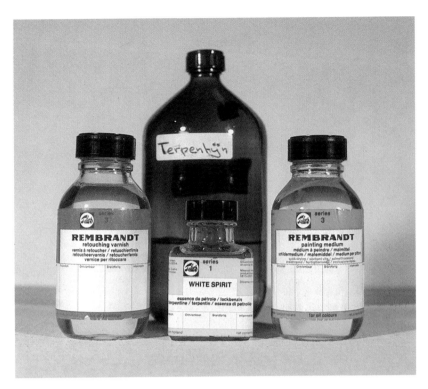

Thinning agents and mediums are auxiliary materials for painting with oils.

THINNING AGENTS

TURPENTINE AND WHITE SPIRIT

In oil painting, turpentine and white spirit are used as thinning agents. Painters' turpentine is a volatile thinning agent which is obtained from the resin of the pine tree. White spirit has the same properties as turpentine and is obtained from the distillation of petroleum.

Turpentine and white spirit are used to thin the oil paint for the application of the first layers, so that an optimum binding between the surface and the paint results. This thin application has the same function as that of an undercoat applied when painting a door, with the difference that the first layers in an oil painting already have form and colour.

After being used in the first layers, these thinning agents must no longer be employed, because the oil paint becomes too thin and cracks (craquelé).

Oil paint loses its butter-like consistency when turpentine and white spirit are used. After the first thin layers have been applied they are replaced by mediums.

MEDIUMS

Various types of medium are available for painting in oils, and each has its own specific property. Thus, there are mediums which slow down or, conversely, speed up the drying process; mediums which thicken or thin the paint; mediums which increase the transparency, and so on.

To prevent confusion, in this first volume of the series we will limit ourselves to two mediums: a liquid medium and a paste medium. The liquid medium is employed in layered painting, the Alla Prima technique and with brushes, while the paste medium is employed in the knife and impasto techniques. The other mediums will be discussed in the third volume of *The Fine Arts Series*.

THINNING AGENTS AND MEDIUMS

Oil paint can be applied straight from the tube, or it can be first made fluid with a thinning agent. Of course, the paint can be thinned with paraffin or benzene, but these liquids are seldom, if ever, used in oil painting and are not to be recommended. Paraffin dries too slowly while benzene is extremely inflammable and evaporates much too quickly for good results to be obtained.

Turpentine and white spirit, which are discussed below, are suitable thinning agents for oil paint.

If a layer of oil paint is applied too sparsely, it can crack on drying and 'craquelure' then appears.

PAINTING MEDIUM *Rembrandt* painting medium (Talens) is prepared from vegetable oils and non-yellowing synthetic resins which are dissolved in, among other things, white spirit. In contrast to turpentine and white spirit, painting medium does not thin the paint. It prevents the forming of cracks, heightens the gloss, and ensures that the butter-like consistency of the paint is not lost too quickly. *Rembrandt* painting medium does not influence the drying time of the paint and can be thinned with turpentine or white spirit if necessary.

These thinning agents are also suitable for cleaning the materials with which the painting medium is used.

PAINTING PASTE *Rembrandt* painting paste (Talens) is also prepared from vegetable oils and non-yellowing synthetic resins. This medium contains thickening agents. It is a colourless paste which does not thin the paint, as long as a proportion of one part paint to three parts painting paste is adhered to. (If necessary, painting paste can be thinned with a little turpentine or white spirit.) In this proportion, fairly thick layers of paint can be applied without the paint wrinkling while it is drying.

Wrinkling occurs during the drying process when the layers of paint have been applied too thickly. When mixed with oil paint, painting paste accelerates the drying process. Due to the very paste-like consistency of the medium, brush strokes and knife strokes remain clear. White spirit is suitable for cleaning the materials with which the painting paste is used.

RETOUCHING VARNISH

Retouching varnish is prepared from colourless resins. It is used as an intermediate varnish and not as a finishing varnish.

An oil painting has a long drying time and a finishing varnish can only be applied when the paint has dried through completely. To protect the paint during this long drying time against dust and the effects of the weather, a coat of retouching varnish can be applied as soon as the paint has dried a little. Usually, this can be done after one or two months. The paint can still breathe under the retouching varnish so that the drying process continues, albeit rather more slowly. When retouching varnish is used in this way, it must be applied very thinly. Retouching varnish gives a silky gloss.

This varnish can also be applied to those areas where, during painting, the surface absorbs more paint than it does elsewhere. This can be very annoying, because the colours are no longer bright and therefore less easy to distinguish. Such areas are treated with varnish, brushed on with a soft-haired spalter (ox hair, for example). The spalter is cleaned with white spirit.

Aerosol sprays are also available, and their use for this purpose can be recommended as there is less chance of damaging the wet paint surface. (Painting can continue a few hours after a surface has been treated in this way.)

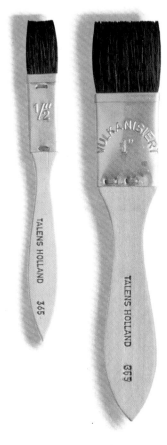

Soft, ox hair spalters are suitable for applying retouching varnish.

SUPPLEMENTARY MATERIALS

Before you begin painting you must ensure that, other than your regular painting materials, you have to hand all the things you will require during your work.

Nothing is more tiresome than having to keep breaking off to go and look for things you need. The best idea is to keep these supplementary materials together in a small chest or strong box.

These materials are:

a piece of charcoal to make sketches,
a screw-top jar for white spirit,
a screw-top jar for turpentine,
a screw-top jar for painting medium,
a coffee filter and filter papers for filtering dirty white spirit,
a large screw-top jar for collecting used thinning agents,
a few cotton cloths, and
soft soap for cleaning your brushes.

LOOKING AFTER YOUR MATERIALS

Keep your painter's box well organized. This prevents rummaging about in a disorganized heap of half-squeezed tubes.

Oil painting materials are expensive, and it is essential from the beginning to look after them properly.

OIL PAINTS   When squeezing paint from the tube, squeeze from the bottom and not from the top. Clean the screw thread on the neck with a cloth before you screw the top back on. Paint remnants 'glue', as it were, the top to the tube and if you apply too much force when you try to open the tube again, the thread can be damaged. If the top does get stuck, warm it in hot water or over a heat source such as a stove or a radiator. Do not heat the top over a naked flame, like a match or a cigarette lighter, as this can melt it!

After using the paint, squeeze what is left in the tube to the top and roll the tube up – in the same way as you roll up your toothpaste tube. Keep your paintbox organized so that you do not have to rummage through a pile of half-used tubes of paint to find a particular colour.

BRUSHES   Oil painting brushes are cleaned with white spirit. Do not leave the brushes too long in the white spirit, because in the long term the enamel on the metal and the glue which binds the hairs can dissolve. Soft-haired brushes will also lose their shape.

After working, first squeeze any excess paint out of the brush hairs with a tissue. Do this from the sleeve towards the end of the hairs so that these are not damaged. Rinse the brushes clean in white spirit and dry them carefully with a cloth. Then wash them with soft soap and lukewarm water in the palm of your hand and rinse them thoroughly in water to get rid of all traces of saop.

·Used thinning agents can be filtered a few times after which they can be re-used.

Store the brushes in a jar with the hairs upwards.

PALETTE AND PAINTING KNIVES   Do not allow paint remnants to dry. Wipe the knives clean with a cloth and then rub them with white spirit.

PALETTE   Clean the area of the palette on which you mixed your colours with white spirit. Remaining quantities of paint can be saved for up to a few days, depending on the temperature and the amount of paint remaining, After that, the drying process is too far advanced and a skin forms on the paint. The palette can be covered with plastic foil to slow down the drying process a little. Hardened paint remnants are scraped off with a palette knife or, if necessary, a paint scraper. If the palette contains very old paint remnants, it is difficult to scrape them off without damaging the palette. To soften them, warm these remnants over a naked flame (a camping gas stove, for example) and then scrape them off. Do this outdoors and use a very low flame so that neither paint nor palette are burnt. Wipe the palette clean with turpentine and rub in a little linseed oil.

THINNING AGENTS AND MEDIUMS   Do not use all your store of thinning agents and mediums at the same time, but pour some into small screw-top jars so that the remainder stays clean. Do not throw dirty turpentine or white spirit away, but save it in a jar or small jerrycan. These materials can be filtered and re-used. (This filtering is done using a funnel-shaped coffee filter and filter papers.)
    Most of the paint particles will remain in the filter paper. Allow the filtered liquid to stand for a few hours so that any remaining paint particles sink to the bottom. Carefully pour the liquid into a jar, taking care not to disturb the sediment. If it is particularly dirty, it can be filtered a second time. The filtered thinning agent is now ready for re-use.
    If the white spirit is still not clean

enough to be used as a thinning agent, it will certainly be good enough to use for cleaning brushes. After a period of time, the white spirit will be so saturated with paint particles that it will no longer be usable. Do *not* pour it down the sink or the toilet, but take it to a garage where there will be a special pit for products of this sort. These pits are regularly emptied by specialist companies and their contents are broken down so that they are not damaging to the environment.

STORING PAINTING MATERIALS

Storing your everyday painting materials in your house should not present too many problems. Paint, thinning agents, mediums and varnishes must not be stored in a cold place. At low temperatures, paint thickens and although the thinning agents and mediums will not freeze, they will become flat and opaque. This can be remedied by allowing them to stand for a few hours at room temperature.

Storing wet working surfaces and trial pieces, however, may present more of a problem. Sooner or later these have to be stored, certainly if you do not have a studio at your disposal.

Oil paintings on paper can be stored against a wall, but hard surfaces need more space. They need a dust-free place to dry, a place which is not too cold or damp and where, moreover, there is enough room for the canvasses to dry separately from each other.

A number of canvasses can be placed together if you use separators. These are available in different forms. Double-headed drawing pins made of synthetic materials or metal, are particularly suit-able for this purpose. They have metal points which you can set into the corners of your piece of work. Because there are points on both the top and the bottom, several canvasses can be stacked on top of each other without them touching. Separators are also available in the form of clips. These are most suitable for storing large canvasses, for which drawing pins are too light. Using clips ensures that the surfaces do not touch and even thickly applied paint will not be damaged.

Ordinary clothes pegs, clipped to the corners, can be used as an alternative for storing thin, hard surfaces. Take care, however, not to damage the paint.

Painting fluids can become 'blind' in low temperatures.

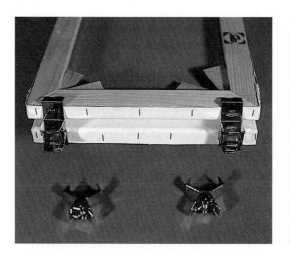

Use separating clips for large surfaces. Double-pointed drawing pins are not sturdy enough for this purpose.

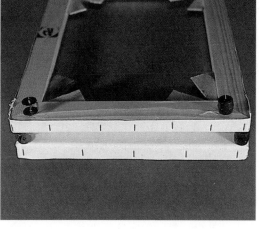

Place a double-pointed drawing pin at each corner of your surface and lay the second surface on the protruding metal points.

Double-pointed drawing pins are simple devices to prevent canvasses laid next to each other from touching.

WHERE TO WORK

Do not sit too close, or too far away, from your subject, but ensure that you have a good view of the subject as a whole without too many surrounding objects to distract you.

You will work indoors or outdoors, depending on the possibilities open to you and your personal preference.

WORKING INDOORS

Determining the place where you will paint is heavily influenced by the space available. Will you work, for example, in your living room at a table easel, or do you have separate studio space at your disposal? In the first case you will probably work sitting, in the second you can decide for yourself whether you will work sitting or standing.

Light is important when painting. Try to position yourself in such a way that if you are right-handed the light falls on the working surface from the left, and if you are left-handed, from the right. This prevents irritating shadows being cast on your painting. Never work in strong sunlight as this has a dazzling effect which influences your colour perception. If you work several times on one painting, always choose the same time of day to work, so that the light is more or less the same.

Not only sunlight, but also artificial light has an influence on colours. Yellow, particularly, is partly neutralised optically, which means that all the colours containing yellow are also changed by artificial light. Apart from the yellows these are the greens, the oranges and some of the reds. This effect can be neutralised by using a daylight lamp while you are working. These are available in the form of ordinary bulbs or as fluorescent tubes.

Do not sit too far away from your subject, because then you cannot see it clearly and also the eye is distracted by surrounding objects. Neither should you sit too close, because then you do not have an overall view of the subject.

Remember that the horizon line is at eye level, whether you are sitting or standing. Depending on the relative positions of the painter and the subject, we

Depending on the position you take up in relation to the subject, you look straight at it, up to it, or down on it.

look directly at the subject, up at it or down on it.

The horizon line follows us; the subject comes to lie above, on or under it.

WORKING OUTDOORS

If you wish to paint outdoors, it is wise to look for your subject beforehand. This way, you do not have to carry your painting materials from one place to another. You also have a chance to observe your subject thoroughly.

When working outdoors you should try to avoid choosing a position in the sun. In any event, ensure that the sunlight does not fall directly on your working surface because that can be fatiguing. It is important always to keep the horizon line precisely in mind, because this determines the way in which you see the subject – are you looking directly at it, down on it, or up to it?

This also determines the relationship between the areas of sky and land in your painting, to give but one example. Nor should you forget to study the colours of your subject. It is important to carry out your observation and the actual

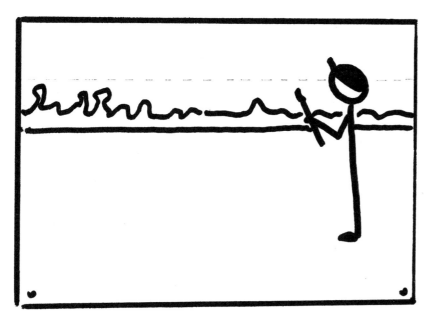

Whether sitting or
standing, your horizon
always lies at eye level.

painting at the same time of day, because the light – and therefore the colours – changes rapidly.

This means that you can only work for a limited number of hours every day. The changing light does not only influence the colours, but the shadows change, too. The later in the day, the longer the shadows. Do not, therefore, continue painting for too long; it is better to resume work at the same time on a different day. Subjects such as colour, composition and perspective will be discussed in depth in the second volume of this series.

Work out beforehand the minimum amount of materials you need to have with you when you work outdoors. Do not take too much!

You need: paint and a few brushes, white spirit and painting medium, a palette or a strip-off palette, a working surface, a piece of charcoal, double-headed drawing pins or separator clips, an extra covering plate or sheet and your easel. Brushes can be protected by rolling them in a cloth or putting them in a brush case. Do not carry your thinning agents and painting medium in glass jars which can easily be broken, but use jars made from synthetic acid-resistant material. If you have no easel, you can use the covering plate for the working surface as a support. Take a small stool if necessary. Nowadays there are handy contraptions available in the shops which enable you to transport your portfolio or working surface easily.

When working outdoors, do not work to a large format. The weather can always play tricks on you. Large working surfaces catch a lot of wind. Moreover, a large surface may have to be worked on a number of times and therefore must be transported frequently. It is better to make small studies of the subject and work them out in a large format at home.

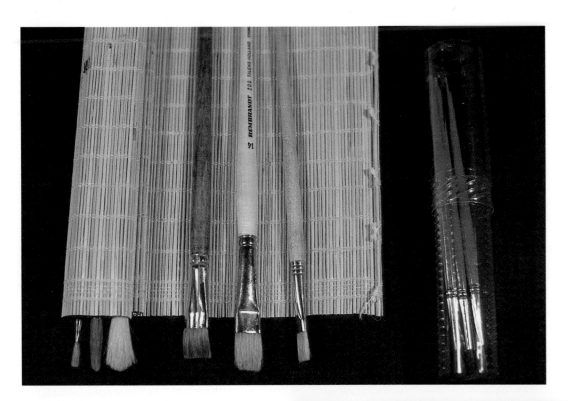

Brushes can be protected by rolling them in a cloth or putting them in a brush case.

A simple solution for carrying your portfolio or working surface.

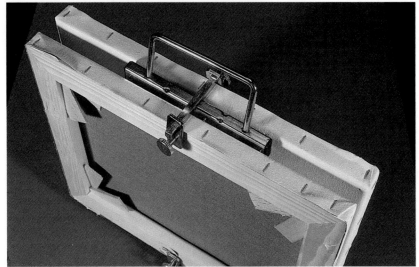

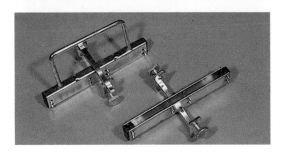

Portable separating clips: an expensive possession?

THE NATURE OF OIL PAINT

NAMES OF COLOURS

Colours were given names at an early stage in history as a result of which colours and their names became associated with each other and a 'colour language' developed. The word 'blue', for example, immediately creates an image in your mind. It invokes your perception.

The more experiences you have acquired, the greater the perception and the greater the power of the images. If one speaks to a child of the concept 'woods', that child's concept, and therefore his impression of the word 'woods', will be associated with the kind of woods of which he has experience, woods where he has been or of which he has seen pictures. An adult has a much wider range of experiences. For him, the concept 'woods' contains much more: large, small, dark, oppressive, cool, terrifying, restful, and so on. We react to the names of colours in a similar way. The word 'blue' therefore conjures up an impression of a colour in the manifestations in which we have experienced it.

If we wish to use a particular colour, then we must first know the name of the colour, or the names of the colours from which we can create the colour concerned. As more and more colour agents (dyes) were discovered over the centuries, the need for a nomenclature in order to denote a particular colour became greater. The names of colours can often be traced to the names of the places where certain minerals were first discovered, and also to the vegetable or animal origins.

Other colours owe their name to the metallic compound from which they are made or carry the name of their creator.

Sienna, an earth colour, owes its name to Sienna, the city in Italy near which

the original earth was discovered. Zinc white bears the name of the metal from which it is made through a process of oxidation. Madder lake and indigo, both vegetable pigments, owe their names to plants, while ivory black is an animal pigment. Some tints are named after artists who regularly used a particular colour in their work. Van Dyck brown is an example of this.

Paint manufacturers also give their own name to particular colours: Talens red (Talens), Oudhollands yellow (Oudt Hollandse Olieverven Makerij Scheveningen), Winsor green (Winsor and Newton), for example. This nomenclature can be confusing. Ask your paint supplier for the shade cards of different companies so that you can compare colours and make your own.

As a rule there is no uniform price for oil paints, because the price depends on the cost of the pigment the paint contains. The cadmium yellows and reds and the cobalt blues and purples, for example, are much more expensive than the earth colours such as sienna and umber, and also more expensive than the blacks and whites.

The basic assortment is a starting assortment in which particular colours can always be replaced. If you specialize in subjects such as portrait or landscape painting, this assortment can always be widened to include specific colours which are indispensable to these subjects.

TRANSPARENCY AND OPACITY

Not all oil paint colours have the same opacity. Depending on the pigment used, a particular colour can be opaque, semi-opaque, semi-transparent or transparent.

Talens manufactures tubes which are coded to indicate the transparency, opacity and lightfastness of the paint.

In the glazing technique, for example, the use of transparent or semi-transparent paint is a prerequisite, because this technique consists of building up transparent layers of paint. In this case, the more the paint is thinned, the more transparent it is.

For the covering of the different layers, such as is done in layered painting, opaque and semi-opaque types of paint are necessary, though transparent paints are also used in this technique.

LIGHTFASTNESS

Lightfastness of the oil paint is important for the preservation of the painting. If we assume a good quality paint, we distinguish between complete, reasonable and moderate lightfastness. When mixed with white, reasonably and moderately lightfast paints – under normal lighting conditions – will in the long term (approximately 10 to 20 years) begin to decline in colour intensity. When two colours of the same degree of lightfastness are mixed, the colour value remains unchanged.

A completely lightfast colour mixed with a colour of a lesser degree of lightfastness assumes the colour value of the lesser. A reasonably lightfast colour mixed with white acquires a moderate degree of lightfastness.

CODING

In this first chapter of this book we began with an assortment of Rembrandt professional oil paints, manufactured by Talens.

There is nothing to prevent you, however, from beginning with students' paints (Van Gogh – Talens).

Talens indicates the transparency and opacity with the following symbols:

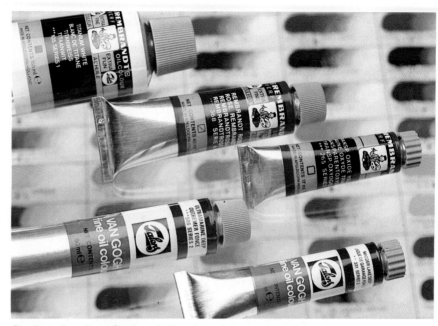

Students' and professional oil paint of the same make can be used in combination.

□ transparent
☒ semi-transparent
◩ semi-opaque
■ opaque

The degree of lightfastness is indicated by plus signs:
+++ highest degree of lightfastness
++ normal degree of lightfastness
+ low degree of lightfastness

The basic assortment thereby carries the following particulars on the tubes:

Colour	Transparency/ opacity	Degree of light-fastness
Cadmium red – light	■	+++
Madder lake – deep	□	++
Cadmium – lemon	■	+++
Cadmium yellow – deep	■	+++
Ultramarine – deep	□	+++
Cobalt blue – light	◩	+++
Cerulean blue	◩	+++
Yellow ochre	■	+++
Burnt sienna	☒	+++
Burnt umber	☒	+++
Ivory black	■	+++
Zinc white	◩	+++

Van Gogh students' paints also carry this code. The quality of these paints, however, sometimes differs from the quality of Rembrandt paints because of the substitution of expensive pigments by pigments which are less expensive.

SETTING OUT THE PALETTE

The oil paints intended for a particular painting are set out along the edge of the palette. The remaining area is used for mixing colours. The paint can be set out in different ways – from light to dark, for example, beginning with white and ending with black. On a left-handed palette the colours are set out from right to left, on a right-handed palette, from left to right.

Another possibility is to set out the colours from yellow to brown, keeping the white and black separate as these are much used for mixing. Relatively speaking, white is used in larger quantities than the colours, and is certainly used more than black. Yet another possibility is to set the colours out in groups; the reds, the yellows, the blues, and so on.

The way in which the palette is set out is very personal. Whichever method you prefer, always stick to the same colour order so that you will become able to find a required colour almost without thinking. Be economical with the paint. It is better to have to add a little paint than to throw it away. Neither is it necessary to set out every colour for each piece of work. The paint which you do not use will dry out and will thus become unusable.

To a large extent, colour mixing is carried out on the palette. Do not mix at random on any arbitrary spot, but work in an orderly fashion and keep the colours together so that the palette remains well-organized.

After working, the area of the palette used for mixing can be cleaned by scraping off the surplus paint with a palette knife and wiping it down with white spirit. You may prefer to leave the mixed colours as they are so that you will have something to refer to. However, the palette should be cleaned regularly: a dirty, disorganized palette affects your work adversely.

Always set your colours in the same order on the palette so that you will soon be able to find a colour almost without thinking.

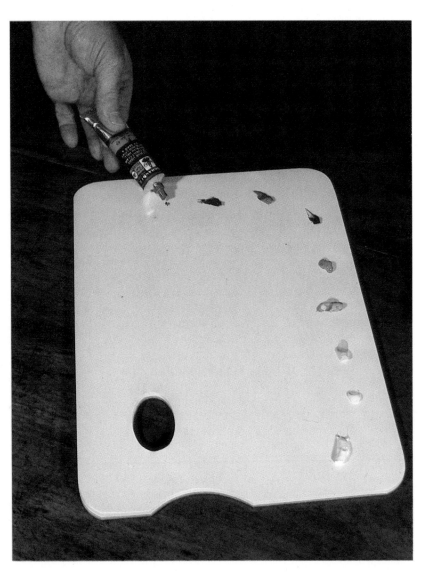

Whichever method you select, always keep your palette well organized.

A disorganized palette has a disturbing effect during painting.

TRYING OUT MATERIALS

TONING DOWN A COLOUR

Paint in the tube has a paste-like consistency. Vivid colours are bright because of the high concentration of pigment and consequently the darker tints have a deep colour.

Oil paint colours can be toned down by mixing them with white paint – preferably with a special mixing white such as zinc white – or by mixing them with a thinning agent or medium.

In the first instance, pastel shades result. The paint retains its consistency and its opacity is increased.

In the second instance, the colour intensity changes less quickly and the colour only becomes lighter after considerable thinning. A well-pigmented paint can be recognized by this. Depending on the degree to which it is thinned, the paint becomes more transparent. The consistency is also affected because the paint is thinner.

The oil paint can be toned down with white spirit or white paint.

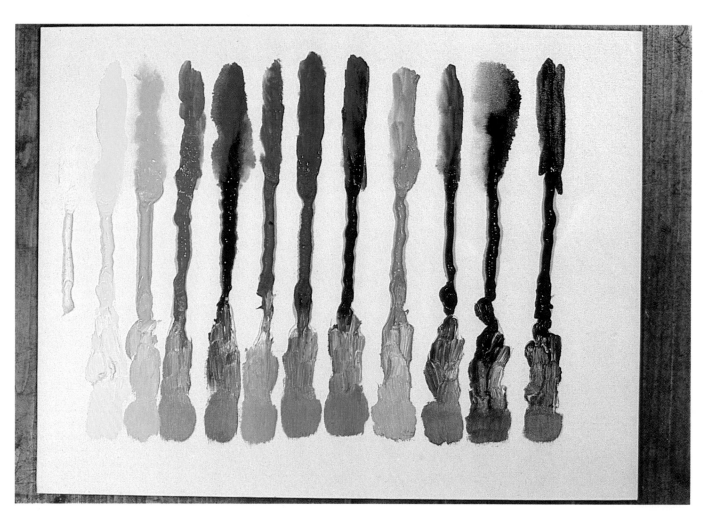

A large colour spectrum can be created from the basic assortment by mixing the colours together.

MIXING COLOURS

It is possible to obtain a wide colour spectrum by mixing together colours from the basic assortment.

Learning to control the mixing of colours is essential in order to obtain the colours which you require and through this your knowledge will be considerably broadened. You will also discover that you develop a preference for certain colours, which will give your work its own character.

Particularly in the beginning, therefore, it is recommended that you mix the colours as often as possible and do not purchase them ready-made. In the second volume of this series the theme of colour will be discussed in greater detail, and therefore we will limit ourselves in this volume to the first principles of mixing.

Red, yellow and blue are primary colours. This means that they are colours which cannot be mixed from other colours.

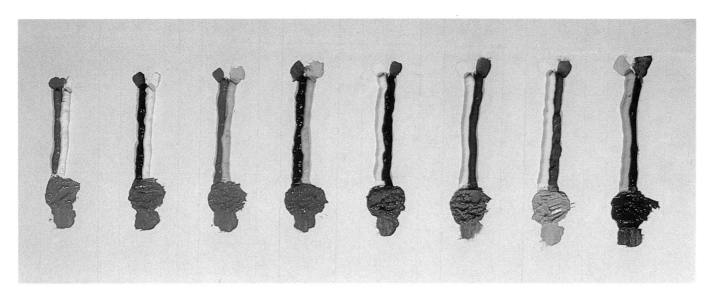

The mixing of two colours from basic assortment I.

Orange, green and violet are secondary colours. They are produced by mixing together primary colours. Red mixed with yellow gives an orange; yellow mixed with blue gives a green; and red mixed with blue gives a violet. The nature of the red, yellow and blue influences the nature of the orange, green and violet. Moreover, the proportions in which they are mixed also modifies the resulting secondary colour.

Colours which are obtained by mixing secondary colours are known as tertiary colours. The three primary colours are always present in a tertiary colour. Orange and violet are both secondary colours. When mixed together they produce a brown. This brown contains the three primary colours. The orange is produced from the primary colours red and yellow, and the violet from the primary colours blue and red.

For pure, clear mixed colours which appear in the spectrum we start with magenta, lemon yellow and cyan. Magenta (red) and cyan (blue) are printers' colours.

As the nature of the mixed colour depends on the nature of the primary colours, it is obvious that, for example, cobalt blue mixed with cadmium lemon gives a completely different green from ultramarine mixed with cadmium yellow deep.

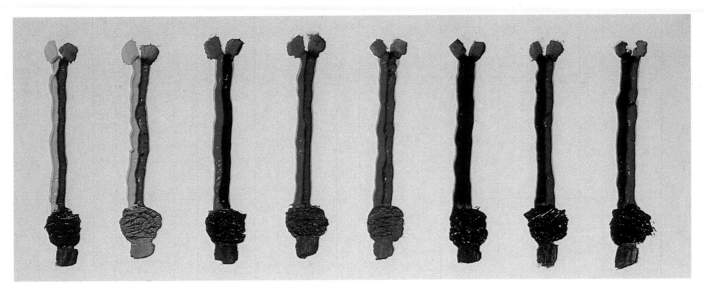

The mixing of two colours from basic assortment II.

Mixing together colours from the basic assortment yields the following colours:

1 Cadmium red – light
  Cadmium lemon

2 Madder lake – deep
  Cadmium lemon

3 Cadmium red – light
  Cadmium yellow – deep

4 Madder lake – deep
  Cadmium yellow – deep

5 Cadmium lemon
  Ultramarine – deep

6 Cadmium lemon
  Cobalt blue – light

7 Cadmium lemon
  Cerulean blue

8 Cadmium yellow – deep
  Ultramarine – deep

9 Cadmium yellow – deep
  Cobalt blue – light

10 Cadmium yellow – deep
   Cerulean blue

11 Cadmium red – light
   Ultramarine – deep

12 Cadmium red – light
   Cobalt blue – light

13 Cadmium red – light
   Cerulean blue

14 Madder lake – deep
   Ultramarine – deep

15 Madder lake – deep
   Cobalt blue – light

16 Madder lake – deep
   Cerulean blue

A completely different series of colours is produced by mixing a colour with white or black.

THE INFLUENCE OF BRUSHES ON OIL PAINT

THE TEXTURE OF STIFF AND SOFT BRUSHES

Painting with oil paints begins with trying out the materials. This is necessary in order to learn their properties. The more you experiment, the better prepared you will be when you eventually begin to paint.

What are the properties of oil paint? What effect has a particular brush on the paint? What is the function of a medium added to the paint? These are all questions which can only be answered after fundamental trials with the materials, trials which you must undertake yourself. In short, knowing 'how to do it' is essential before the making of a piece of work.

THE BRUSHSTROKE

The type of brush determines the form of the brushstroke, and whether a painting medium is used or not influences the texture, or structure, of the stroke.

For the following experiments use a material such as oil painting paper. Make a thin underpainting in a fairly dark colour, well-thinned with white spirit. This ensures that the experiments with a lighter-coloured paint will be successful. White spirit evaporates quickly. About half an hour after the underpainting has been applied, it will have dried sufficiently and the experiments can begin.

I For the first experiment use a broad flat Gussow. Thin a light-coloured oil paint with a little painting medium. Make a few brushstrokes on your working surface. This type of brush gives a broad stroke with a linear structure.

II The side of the flat Gussow can also be used. The strokes are then narrower but they still retain their linear structure.

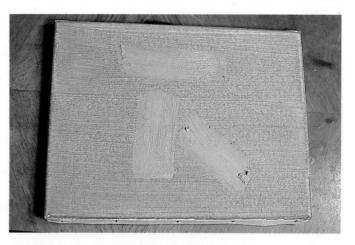

III Both narrow and broad strokes can be made with a round Gussow, depending on the pressure you apply to the brush. The characteristic of this brushstroke is the rounded structure, as opposed to the linear structure of that of the flat Gussow.

IV The texture can be influenced by varying the amount of painting medium added to the oil paint. In a stroke applied with paint which is barely thinned, the marks of the brush hairs remain visible. An ox hair brush gives a softer structure than a stiff hog's hair brush.

V Adding more medium makes the paint run more freely. An ox hair brush gives a smoother colour stroke than a hog's hair brush.

VI It is also possible to vary the amount of paint taken up by the brush so that, according to the requirements, full, or only thin, dry strokes of colour are applied.

REPETITION OF THE BRUSHSTROKE
Brushstrokes are repeated in a painting. They are placed next to, and on top of, each other. Depending on the painting technique chosen, this is carried out layer over layer, with or without a period of drying time between the application of the layers.

In the first instance the paint does not mix with the underlying layers, which is the usual case with layered painting.

In the second instance the colours do mix with the still-wet layers, which is the case when the Alla Prima technique is employed.

If you are going to carry out experiments, then you can do several of them in the two techniques. The difference between them will then be clearly seen. Remember when experimenting with the layered painting technique that each layer must first dry out before another is applied. This can take several days for each layer.

Colour all the surfaces on which you will make colour trials.

I Using a broad, flat Gussow, lay down a layer of paint by applying a number of stripes. When this is dry, apply a second and third layer in the same way. The paint does not mix with the paint of the underlying layers.

III Using a flat, not too broad, Gussow, one after the other while the paint is still wet. The wet layers mix.

III Using a flat, not too broad, Gussow, build up a layer of paint in small, short planes. Change the direction of the brushstroke occasionally. Allow the layer to dry and then apply two more layers in the same way. The paint does not mix with the underlying layers.

IV Repeat experiment III, but apply the layers one after the other while the paint is still wet. The wet layers mix.

V Using a thin, round Lyons brush, apply a layer of paint in short and long narrow brushstrokes. Use different colours. Try to bring some texture to the work by changing the direction of the brushstroke a few times. Let the paint layer dry. Repeat this procedure twice.

VI Again using a thin, round Lyons brush, repeat experiment V. Apply the layers one after the other without allowing the layers to dry. The layers of paint mix together. The object here is not to spread the paint too much so that the colours remain bright.

VII Using a round Lyons brush, apply a layer of paint in lively brushstrokes using different colours. Allow the layer to dry and repeat this procedure twice. The paint layers do not mix.

VIII Conduct a similar experiment to No VII, but do not allow the layers to dry. The paint strokes mix together. Try to maintain the colour difference.

IX Layered painting can also be combined with the wet-on-wet technique. Allow some areas to dry before you paint over them. Now use the wet-on-wet technique. In this experiment a fine, round brush is used. In this case the underpainting is sparsely applied, and after drying it is further painted with thinned-down paint. The shrubs and the grass are laid down without a drying period in between.

X For this experiment, the paint is thinned with painting medium. A soft brush is used. There are three layers and each is allowed to dry before the next is applied, The brushstrokes have partly run together, while in other areas they are still visible.

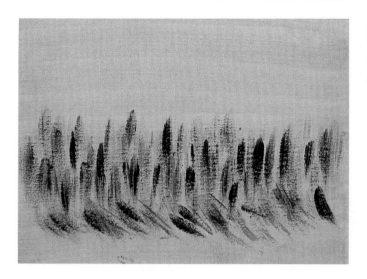

XI For this last experiment use a stiff Gussow. Make repeated sweeping strokes with only a very small amount of unthinned paint on the brush, scarcely touching the working surface. This results in dry paint strokes.

BRUSH HANDLING TECHNIQUES OF WELL-KNOWN MASTERS   With the experience you have acquired from the foregoing experiments, you will probably be able to recognize the brush handling techniques used in certain paintings. Use a magnifying glass so that you can see the detail better.

The Silver Tree – 1912
PIET MONDRIAAN

In his painting *The Silver Tree*, Piet Mondriaan used the Alla Prima technique. The brushstrokes are clearly visible. He used straight-cut flat Gussows in different sizes. Because the strokes are not all in the same direction, the work has a liveliness and mobility.

Mondriaan limited himself to white, black and greys. Almost all the brush touches have been effected by mixing with the paint already applied to the canvas. Sometimes it appears that he has taken up white and black in one brush.

Compare the technique used here with experiment II in the previous section (page 50).

Mont Sainte-Victoire
– 1904-1906
PAUL CEZANNE

Cézanne built up this painting primarily with short, horizontal brush strokes, but used another structure in the sky.

The construction of the painting can be seen particularly well through a magnifying glass. Certain influences of Cubism can be observed and except for a few areas, details have been omitted. The work has been painted in layers which are not mixed with each other. The colours are beautifully in tune with each other. On closer inspection, the enormously broad colour spectrum of his palette becomes apparent.

*Estate at Sunset:
View From the Hospi-
tal of Saint-Rémy
– 1889*
VINCENT VAN GOGH

Vincent van Gogh was a born Alla Prima painter and he pushed this technique to its furthest limits. He built up his landscape with an endless repetition of colour slashes and continued to do this until the painting was finished.

Notice how he used this structure to follow the undulations of the land. The structure around the setting sun emphasizes its intense glow. There are also structures applied over the dried paint; these have not mixed with the un-

derlying layers of paint. Compare this painting with experiment VI in the previous section (page 51).

Autumn Sky – 1910
EMIL NOLDE

Emil Nolde executed this painting principally in the Alla Prima technique and applied a few more accents after the paint had dried a little. In these areas the paint has not mixed with the underlying layers. It is obvious that he made further additions to the ground and also to the sky.

A blazing sky is created with thick paint. The mixing of colours came about primarily on the canvas itself. The brush handling is extremely mobile. Compare this painting with the lively brush handling in experiment VIII in the previous section (page 52).

L'Estaque – 1882
AUGUSTE RENOIR

Renoir has given his subject a streaky texture. The painting is largely painted in layers. Some additions have been made in the last paint layers where he applied the Alla Prima technique in the small details.

The picture is painted with fairly thin brush strokes. There is a lovely variation in the structures and the direction of these structures.

The painting is completely opaque.

Landscape – 1835
WILLIAM TURNER

This landscape is a layered painting, partly in transparent and partly in opaque layers.

For the transparent layers, the well-thinned paint was applied with soft brushes. Here, the brushstrokes cannot be seen.

The sky consists of layers of opaque paint rubbed or brushed in. It is possible that a palette knife was also used.

Turner was a master in the art of suggesting intense light by applying glazes over opaque layers.

58

On the Shore of Lake Thoune – 1905
FERDINAND HOLDLER

This painting is a good example of the use of the dry brush technique. This technique is applied on a layered surface. The dry brush technique was used in experiment XI in the previous section (page 53).

THE INFLUENCE OF PAINTING KNIVES ON OIL PAINT

Painting knives give the oil paint a completely different texture to that created by the brush stroke. This texture depends on the shape of the knife used and the way in which it is handled.

For experiments in this technique, see 'Knife techniques', page 96.

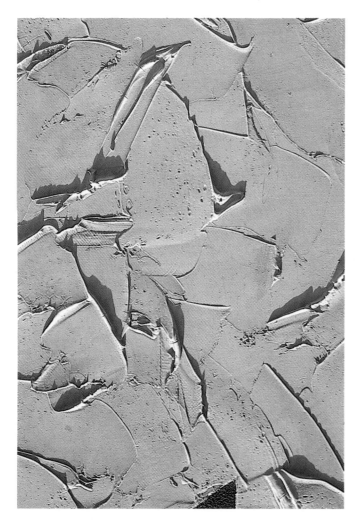

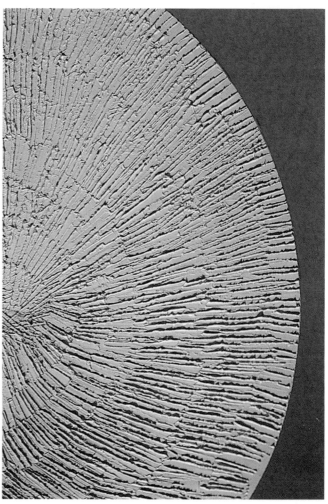

In this experiment a short knife is used. The paint is spread smoothly over the canvas.

This texture was produced with the edge of a long pointed knife.

Painting knives can be used to replace as well as to complement brushes. *The City*, by August Strindberg, provides a good example of this. In the sky, particularly, the brush and the painting knife were applied alternately.

The City
– undated
AUGUST STRINDBERG

THE METHOD OF EXPRESSION

The manner in which you execute a piece of work will depend on a number of factors, such as your individual perception of the subject, your innate talent and the level of ability you have achieved. In the first place it is important that you give expression to what exists inside you, that you arrive at your own means of expression, and do not automatically accept those imposed on you by others.

Drawing methods based on demonstration and imitation encourage clichéd work.

There are still too many drawing manuals from which mannerisms are acquired; in which, for example, we are led to believe that a tree is a cloud or a balloon on a stick or that a fir tree is a triangle on a pole, in which every area and colour is indicated; so that in practice an identical end result is always achieved. These methods are only based on 'rules' and have nothing to do with individual contribution. Expression is not about 'how it has to be', but about 'what do I feel', 'what do I want', 'how do I do it'. It is about producing genuine, honest work, work that contains some-

thing of oneself, personal work, which – because it is personal – does not disappear in the mass, but always remains recognizable.

Once you have learned to handle a particular drawing or painting technique and thoroughly studied subjects such as colour effects and composition – which indeed can contribute to your expression – you will be able to produce high-quality pieces of work which will stand the test of time.

We all need criticism of our work, therefore never ignore it. Always consider if the criticism is constructive as far as *your* work is concerned, and if it is, take advantage of it. Do not forget, however, that criticism is often dictated by a dislike of, or a fear of, a means of expression which appears to deviate from the accepted norms, and that this kind of criticism is often unjustified.

A good example of this is the enormous criticism the Impressionists had to endure when they attempted – not so long ago, about a hundred years – to bring a new aspect to the art of painting.

It concerned a group of largely young painters like Camille Pisarro, Auguste Renoir, Claude Monet, Edouard Manet and Georges Seurat. When they attempted to present their newly acquired ideas to the public they were reviled and mocked, and even rejected by The Salon, the annual exhibition organized by the Académie Française. Their work was regarded as a travesty, an outrage against the standards pertaining at that time. These was indignation at the way in which they paid no attention to the making of a faithful reproduction of the subject. It was thought that their technique had nothing to do with painting and that their works were only 'half-finished'.

One of the reasons for this criticism

Brooklyn Bridge – 1958
Bernard Buffet

Buffet represents the city by an interplay of lines.

was the fact that the Impressionists no longer concerned themselves with the purely academic, but allowed nature, everyday life in all its facets, to influence them, and set down their impressions in countless slashes of colour full of movement and spontaneity. The classical three-dimensional form of painting was sometimes unrecognizable and often disregarded completely. They went out to their subject and painted it 'in situ'. Academic painters, particularly, were extremely irritated by this turn of events. Now we know that they were wrong: Impressionism is one of the best known and most appreciated art movements. The many art movements which followed were also often accompanied by incomprehension and ridicule. Expressionism, abstract art forms such as Cobra, Dada, Pop-art and Super-realism, to name only a few, suffered these reactions. In these movements, painters never stood alone. Sculptors, poets, writers, musicians, architects, dancers, actors were always of like mind, or they were the precursors and therefore the pacemakers. This evolution has continued to this day and is still continuing, with periods of growth, standstill and regression. Many artists have made legendary statements on this subject, statements which were sometimes received with approval, but frequently with indignation.

'I have come to the conclusion that we must go back to nature itself, but not to reproduce it in the way that a photographer tends to do.'
GUILLAUME APOLLINAIRE (1881-1918)

'People's ideas change frequently and with them their means of expression.'
PABLO PICASSO (1881-1973)

'I just mess around', was Karel Appel's irritated answer to a fatuous question about his working methods. It was an expression which amused many, but the 'ignorant' seize on such a statement as proof of their opinion on all this 'modern rubbish'. They do not know what to think of it and therefore scoff at it. Often, the wonderful, clean paintings and drawings of young children, with their characteristic direct rough splashes of colour, shapes and lines, are not appreciated either by these sort of people. They cannot understand them and do not take the trouble to go deeply into the child's desire to express himself.

Brazilian Landscape
– 1925
LASAR SEGALL

Segall used planes
and colours for the
depiction of this
village.

Opponents of the unusual and/or the new
do not understand the why or the how.
They do not understand that a person is
the product of his own time and his own
culture, with his own will, but especially
his own purpose, a purpose which leads
him to a specific form of expression.

Paris – 1920
FILIPPO DE PISIS

De Pisis gives an impression of Paris through suggestion, rather than a precise visual image of the city.

GENERAL PAINTING RULES

Your creativity, your powers of expression and your spontaneity determine the artistic quality of the oil painting you make. In contrast, the durability of the painting depends only on your technical knowledge and how you apply that knowledge. It happens only too often that what appears to be a satisfactory painting deteriorates in the course of time because of various reactions in the paint which were not at first visible. For example, the paint is absorbed to too great an extent, or wrinkles because of uneven drying; the paint prematurely cracks or peels off in places. The instructions in this book should therefore be carefully followed. Bear in mind, however, that there are, naturally, further possibilities. When you have acquired more experience you will have the chance to use other materials and to follow other approaches, but first you must learn about the effect of basic materials, so that you do not become confused. The range of materials will be extended in later volumes.

THE PAINTING PRINCIPLE OF FAT OVER LEAN

When painting in oils, we must always begin with the principle of 'fat over lean' (also called 'oily over less oily').

This means that each paint layer applied must be a little more oily than the previous one in order to ensure a good binding between the layers. Oil paint consists of very finely ground pigments in a vegetable oil which acts as a binding agent. A drying paint layer is porous. If you were to apply two paint layers of the same composition over one another, the first layer would abstract a little oil from the second, which would result in the latter layer being less oily than the first. This can result in crackling during the drying process, particularly if the second layer is thinly applied. Cracks appear in the paint layer, and the paint can even peel off.

In order to prevent this, every paint layer must always be more oily than the previous one. This is achieved by adding painting medium to the paint, or an oil intended for this purpose. For now we will use the painting medium from your stock of basic materials. When oil is used a layer which is prematurely oily may be produced. It is possible to prevent this from happening, but this requires a little more experience. We will therefore discuss this later.

If the first paint layer (the underpainting) is thinned with turpentine or white spirit to create a very thin coating, in principle it is not necessary to add painting medium to the second layer, because the paint for this layer already contains more oil than the thin underlying layer. All the following layers, however, must always be made more oily to allow for the absorption of the oil binding agent from the paint. If the first layer is pure paint, the second layer *must* be made more oily, as must all the following layers.

With every new layer, a little oil is abstracted from it and absorbed by the layer under it, so that this new, uppermost layer in its turn, becomes a little

paint layers

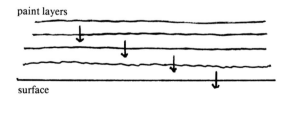

surface

The first layout in charcoal. Do not indicate too many details.

The first layout in oil paint of one colour. A few planes are vaguely indicated.

less oily. It is not necessary, therefore, to add still more medium to each layer: the same quantity will do.

But even when the paint has been made more oily, it can be over-absorbed in places. This can be remedied by covering the affected area with retouching varnish. When this has dried, you can continue painting. When your painting is finished and the paint is somewhat dry, it can be varnished with this retouching varnish. As mentioned earlier, retouching varnish is an intermediate varnish and a finishing varnish can only be applied when the paint has completely dried (see Retouching Varnish, page 32).

FIRST PREPARATIONS

Make a number of preliminary studies on paper with charcoal or pencil before you begin to paint. Consider whether you will later set your working surface vertically or horizontally (a subject containing clear vertical lines often demands a vertical plane, while a subject with horizontal lines is sometimes better executed on a horizontal surface).

As far as possible, try to ensure that the proportions of your sketches are the same as those of your surface. If your surface, for example, has a format of 50 x 60 cm, make your sketches in formats such as 5 x 6 cm, 10 x 12 cm, etc. You then have a better overall idea of what your eventual composition will look like.

The first layout in thinned oil paint in which the main tints are briefly indicated.

Make sure that your surface is well prepared. Prepared surfaces which have stood for a while should be wiped down with a little white spirit to get rid of any possible deposits. Only a grease-free, absorbent surface ensures a good binding with the oil paint.

The sketch can be transferred to the surface in different ways:

with charcoal,

with thinned paint in a single colour,
or

with thinned paint in several colours from your subject.

Whichever method you use, make only a rough sketch and transfer only those details which are necessary for the first phase. None of the remaining details will be needed until the final phase.

If you make a sketch in charcoal, you must wipe away the loose charcoal particles with a feather (duck's wing) or a cotton cloth before you apply the first paint layer. Never do this with your hand because the grease on your skin transfers to the surface and can prevent the paint from binding properly.

The first paint layer can now be applied. Try to set down the whole subject, or in any case the larger part of it, directly in the painting, and do not work in small areas or parts of the subject. If you do this, you lose the overall conception of your piece of work.

LAYERED PAINTING

The layered painting technique is a classic technique which was already frequently used in the early days of painting. In this technique, the paint is applied layer by layer, in a thin or a thicker paint film, and a brush as well as a painting knife can be used. There is always an intermediate drying time between each layer.

This drying period depends on the temperature and the degree of humidity, while the quantity of thinning medium – turpentine, white spirit or painting medium – can also be a determinant.

Basically, layered painting can be carried out with opaque or with transparant paint. Nevertheless there is a distinction between layered painting with largely opaque or semi-opaque paint (in which the underlying paint layers can be com-

A painting knife was used to lay down the paint in the left-hand half of this trial piece, while a brush was used in the right-hand half. The paint is applied opaquely.

The paint can also be applied when thinned, so that it is possible to produce transitions of colour.

pletely or partially covered), and the painting of glazes. Transparent paints are used to a large extent in glazing. Through the application of still more transparent layers of paint, intense colour and depth effects are achieved, and glazing therefore calls for a different paint-handling technique. This technique will be explained in the second volume of *Oil Painting Techniques*.

Paintings in the layered painting technique can therefore be made in different textures. However, they are always built up layer by layer without the layers mixing together.

DESCRIPTION OF TECHNIQUE BASED ON ACTUAL PAINTINGS

Provence – 1986
AD MERX

This sunny picture was made in the French Provence district. It is built up for the most part in vertical slashes of colour laid down on top of each other. The paint is applied thinly.

Nude – 1917
WALTER RICHARD
SICKERT

In this picture the oil paint is applied un-thinned or only slight-ly thinned. It is also a layered painting. Nowhere have the paint layers been mixed.

Donkeys on the Beach – undated
ANTON MAUVE
(1838-1888)

Mauve has laid down clouds over the blue sky and he has partly brushed them over the blue so that colour transitions are pro-duced. In places the blue shimmers through the cloud cover.

Third of May –
1808-1814
FRANCISCO GOYA

This picture is executed in the layered painting technique. At first glance the enormous amount of work put into this world-famous painting by the artist is not apparent.

Only when we examine the detail of the boot and the sabre, can we understand how labour-intensive the making of this painting must have been.
   In the detail (next page, bottom), it can be seen that the strongest light reflections were laid down in the topmost paint layer.

A CLOSER LOOK AT A LAYERED PAINTING

Inanna – 1986
PAUL VERSTEEG

She is Paul Versteeg's daughter and she does not mind posing for him. She tries to do it well, but her thoughts are elsewhere. Versteeg has made a good portrait, but he has done more than that. He has succeeded in capturing what is going on in Inanna's mind. There she stands in her pink jacket and her high-heeled shoes. She does not mind staying, but actually she would prefer to leave. She is standing in the starting blocks, as it were, ready for the off.

For this 'composition in pink', as he calls it, Versteeg used a type of paint containing the very expensive pigment, quinacridone. This transparent oil paint is very intensive in colour and completely lightfast. Because of its high pigmentation, the paint can be well thinned. This degree of lightfastness can not be achieved with madder lake ++ mixed with white +++ (see Lightfastness, page 41).

The artist painted this large picture (120 x 180 cm) in well-thinned paint of which principally the main colours of the jacket and trousers – pink and blue – were mixed with white. The canvas is not completely covered with paint so that in different places its structure is visible through the paint layer. The colours of the background are in tune with the pink colour of the jacket.

DETAILS FROM THE PAINTING

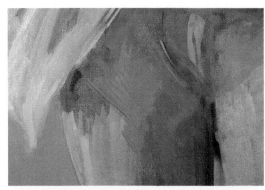

I Because this detail consists of only pink tints, the layered painting technique is clearly observable. All the colours are clearly separate and are built up layer by layer. The lightest tints, which indicate the actual light, are laid down in the last layer.

II Notice the three-dimensional effect of the brushstroke. The colour strokes are not everywhere applied with the same force.

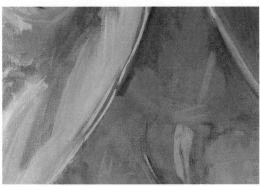

III The effect of depth is heightened by setting light and dark accents next to each other. The greatest degree of light is also laid down on a dark tint.

IV The bracelets accentuate the bulk of the arm. The dark, pure madder lake (unmixed) accents are used to emphasize the areas of light.

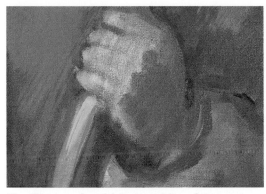

V The way in which the white of the canvas is incorporated is clearly visible in this detail. It draws attention to the fact that the light in this detail is not painted, but is indicated by the unpainted structure of the canvas.

VI The eyes are the darkest part of the painting, and because of this, attention is drawn to the head. Yellow tints are used for the areas of light in the face. This is due to the light also containing a lot of yellow. The pink tint above the eyes and on the lips are an expression of the mascara Inanna used. The fringe was painted last, with extra accents of light.

TRYING OUT MATERIALS: LAYERED PAINTING

I When trying out your materials, decide for yourself which brushes you will use.

Trials can be made with very thin or with moderately thin paint, and also with paint thinned with a small amount of painting medium. Always make a few trials at the same time, because each layer must dry before you can lay down the following layer.

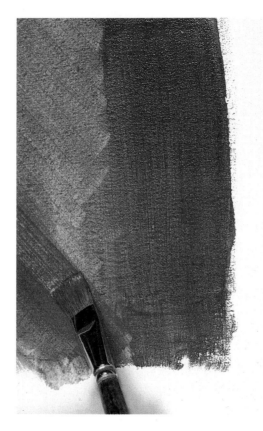

II To indicate light lay down lighter areas over a darker layer.

III Opaque paints cover the underlying layer. After the ochre-coloured paint layer has dried, a red tint is brushed in, so that a colour transition is created. Also use a different type of brush occasionally.

LAYERED PAINTING IN PICTURES
AN ARTIST AT WORK

Paul Versteeg planned to execute two versions of a still life with bottles. However, things turned out rather differently . . .

For his surfaces, Versteeg used high-quality oil-impregnated hardboard called *masonite*, in two formats. The still lifes were executed in the layered painting technique, using Lyons brushes of long Chinese hog's hair.

The surfaces were thoroughly sanded so that all surface irregularities were removed and then prepared with Gesso, applied in vertical and horizontal layers. Because Versteeg wanted a very smooth surface for these still lifes – so he could apply the paint very thinly – he also sanded each layer of primer completely smooth. When preparing his surfaces, Versteeg always finishes with a horizontally applied layer. This way he avoids problems with the spalter strokes, which always remain visible when he is painting with well-thinned paint and there is a particular fall of light on the surface.

The artist begins by arranging the bottles, an important part of the process which will lead to the finished paintings.

Two groupings were chosen: a group of three bottles on the left and a group of two bottles on the right.

Versteeg first makes a few preliminary studies to explore the possibilities of composition and form.

THE FIRST VERSION OF THE STILL LIFE

Still Lifes – 1987
PAUL VERSTEEG

I The first design is laid down in thinned oil paint. The composition is determined using the preliminary studies as a point of departure. The definitive choice is made.

II The first colour separations are made, working over the whole area. Although apparently brown, yellow and blue tints are used, the colours can be classified in three 'families': the reds (from which the brown originates), the yellows and the blues.

Never work in small areas, because you then immerse yourself in the details of the subject and lose sight of the painting as a whole.

The paint is still being used sparingly. The bottle at the back on the right is still not clearly defined, as if the artist is having doubts.

III The paint is now used a little less sparingly, but the artist is still applying it thinly and smoothly. The effects of the areas of colour are strengthened. Areas of light and shadow are indicated. It is as if the bottle at the back on the right is not actually included in the painting.

IV Something has happened here! Another bottle has disappeared! One of the characteristic possibilities of layered painting is that areas the artist does not like, for whatever reason, can be painted out. By painting out the bottle, the composition has undergone a readjustment and has become more restful.

V On a later visit to the studio, it appears that Versteeg has painted out all the bottles and replaced them with a completely new composition – a cloth, a bowl and a funnel!

The artist gave the following explanation for this: 'I was working on two paintings of the same subject and I discovered that I liked the second version, painted on a taller, narrower surface, better than the first. The vertical lines of the bottles show up much better. In the other version the bottles formed a barrier. This horizontal composition works better for this surface, it creates a sense of space.'

X-ray research on paintings by famous masters has brought to light the fact that under them lie not only certain differences in detail, but indeed sometimes completely different pictures.

THE SECOND VERSION OF THE STILL LIFE
After it had been prepared, the surface
was given an ochre tinted layer. This
layer was applied very sparingly, with
paint thinned with white spirit. (Technical name for this: *imprimatur*.)

I Here, too, the subject is laid down in thinned oil paint, while the darkest area is indicated immediately. The composition differs
slightly from the first version. The table is
no longer placed at the edge of the picture
and there is more space in the foreground.

II The painting is carried out more quickly
because of the experience acquired during
the work on the first version. Here, too, the
bottle at the back on the right is barely indicated. The colours in this painting are notice-
ably warmer than in the first because of the
ochre-coloured imprimatur and the influence
of the reds and yellows.

III Here a few colour revisions are made and accents applied. The yellow floor area has become a little softer in colour.

IV Through a continual observation of the subject, an interaction arises between it, the artist and the painting. Increasing amounts of oil are added to the paint.

V Because of the latter format, the vertical lines of the bottles are not disturbing. In this painting, they are even strengthened by the vertical lines of the table leg and by the lines in the background. In this last phase, accents of light and shadow particularly are added. Because these are laid down side by side, they reinforce each other.

THE WET-ON-WET TECHNIQUE

Omar Talon – 1602
PHILIPPE DE CHAMPAIGNE

An intense, deep colour is achieved by continually laying down thin, often transparent, layers of paint one over the other.

Choirboy – 1928
CHAIM SOUTINE

New pigments of high colour density make it possible to achieve a deep, bright colour in the first paint layers.

The wet-in-wet (or wet-on-wet) technique, which is also referred to as *Alla Prima* (the first time) and *Au premier coup* (the first stroke), is one of the direct painting techniques. Alla Prima was already known at the end of the 17th century, but was used infrequently. Only in the 19th century did it become a common technique, although even then it was not always immediately accepted. Due to developments in the oil paint industry more and more durable and intense pigments were used to produce paste-like oil paint and partly because of this it became possible to achieve a strong colour in the first applied layer of paint. Previously, such strength of colour could only be achieved by the application of several, usually transparent, layers of paint (through optical effect).

In contrast to layered painting, which has already been described, and glazing, which will be discussed in the next volume of this series – both techniques in which the application of several layers of paint, always with an intermediate drying period, is necessary to produce the finished painting – the Alla Prima technique is a method which leads directly to the final result. An Alla Prima painting is usually completed in one sitting, with at the most a few highlights being added later.

This means that the subject to be painted is captured directly on the canvas, and that after the first thin layer of paint every brushstroke is applied on the already laid-down, still-wet layers of paint.

Mixing of the colours in the layers only comes about through the wet brushstrokes in the still-wet underlying layers. This gives rise to the term 'wet-on-wet'. Besides composition, colour and form, the texture of the paint and the brush, therefore, play a very important role. The characteristics of the wet-on-wet technique are power, expressiveness and accuracy.

DESCRIPTION OF TECHNIQUE BASED ON ACTUAL PAINTINGS

Berthe Morisot demonstrates that the wet-on-wet technique, just like the classic painting techniques, can also be used to create atmospheric pictures. The soft colour shades are due to a well-balanced palette and the way in which the artist has laid down the areas of light and shadow – in fairly rough brushstrokes with paste-like paint over a sparsely applied underpainting – has resulted in a subtle, intimate painting. The barely visible strip of wall on the right of the painting accentuates the depth of the room and at the same time heightens the atmosphere of intimacy. The paint is not laid down with equal thickness over the entire painting, and in some places the structure of the linen is visible.

The Dining Room –
1884
BERTHE MORISOT

*Singer at a Café
Concert* – 1880
EDOUARD MANET

Manet often used the wet-on-wet technique for his paintings in the variety theatre. The speed of this technique was most suitable in allowing him to capture theatrical events as they happened.

The invention of the portable metal tube in the middle of the 19th century increased the range of vision of many painters. Where previously they had been tied to their studios by their classic painting methods and by their materials, they were now able to take their tubes of paste-like paint with them and paint outside. It is not surprising that methods of direct painting developed rapidly from that moment on.

The 'plein-air' Impressionist painters, in particular, experimented with this paint and used the strength of its colour and its structural possibilities in their work.

In clear, varied and rhythmic brushstrokes, Van Gogh captured form, light and space. He always laid down his paint touches in rich colour.

Clear, directly applied lines and touches of colour took the place of the slow building techniques of the classic painting methods such as layered painting and glazing.

Among other things, the direct painting techniques demanded a high skill from the Impressionist landscape painters. Inspired as they were by the rapidly changing light, it was necessary to work quickly and directly in order to capture the quality of that light. Each artist, therefore, acquired his own personal style.

In Impressionist, Expressionist and abstract art the structural properties of oil paint continue to play an important role.

Vincent Van Gogh is an example of a painter who exploited the possibilities of oil paint to their full, and his many Alla Prima paintings bear witness to this.

Street in Auvers
– 1890
VINCENT VAN GOGH

Street in Auvers
– 1890 (detail)
VINCENT VAN GOGH

From the detail of this painting it appears that nowhere did Van Gogh intentionally mix his paint. The brushstrokes are clearly deliberate, in the knowledge of what effect a particular stroke of colour would produce.

The wet-on-wet technique is not a simple one. The direct application of paint in the right place, and the mixing of colours only by laying down paint strokes over underlying, still-wet, paint strokes – without changing the stroke by rubbing or brushing – not only demands a great deal of technical knowledge but also requires a spontaneous method of working. Only when it is known beforehand what effect a particular paint stroke will have on the form, colour and the structure, can this impulsive method of working be exploited to its full.

The Jay's Nest – 1986
JACQIE VINK

The Jay's Nest is the expression of Jacqie Vink's powerful protest against the shooting of jays in order to protect the biological balance. The artist is someone who very much wants to believe that nature is capable of keeping itself in balance.

For her still life she laid the dead birds next to each other on a white cloth and then marked them, as it were, with a row of spent cartridge cases. It is as though the Flemish jay in the foreground is nestling its already lifeless body between the dead bodies of the magpies. In this way Jacqie Vink captures the corpses, between light and dark, in strong, aggressive brushstrokes: an indictment. In the application of the wet-on-wet technique, the paint was not thinned, or only slightly thinned, so that the brushstrokes remain visible. Stiff hog's hair Gussows were used.

One of the greatest dangers when using the wet-on-wet technique is that there is a chance of 'killing' the colours. This occurs through too much mixing of the wet paint layers or through the wrong use of colour. Muddy colours result, colours which are no longer interesting and which give the painting a drab appearance.

It is therefore important that you master the art of mixing of colours. You must know beforehand what effect the application of a colour will have on an underlying wet layer.

In *The Jay's Nest*, Jacqie Vink has managed to keep her subject clearly defined and the paint and texture interesting, despite the use of a great deal of white and black, colours which can certainly degenerate into a muddy mess.

Lovers in Space – 1954
ASGER JORN

In this painting, Asger Jorn has also used colours which were not created by mixing with the underlying layers.

They were mixed on the palette and applied to the canvas in one layer. This is clearly visible, particularly in the faces of both figures. Jorn used thick paint in this Alla Prima painting.

In the texture of the hair you can see that several layers of paint have been applied. In the left-hand figure, the paint has mixed with the underlying layers. In the hair of the right-hand figure, the lighter underlying layer has become visible through scratching the paint with the end of the brush (or fingernails?).

The picture was probably painted with stiff brushes, though it is also possible that it was made by means of *finger-painting*. The texture is strengthened in various places by scratches in the wet paint.

TRYING OUT MATERIALS: THE WET-ON-WET TECHNIQUE

The wet-on-wet technique is learned in the same way as the other techniques discussed so far: by experimenting with the materials.

For this a piece of prepared board or card is used. Oil painting paper is less suitable for this technique because the paint is often applied thickly which means that after drying, if the paper is bent, the paint can crack.

A possible solution is to glue the oil painting paper to a solid surface.

The Alla Prima technique can also be carried out with painting knives, but here we use stiff hog's hair Gussows where the paint is applied thickly, and ox hair brushes where the paint is applied less thickly. (The texture is then somewhat less structured.)

Apply a thin underpainting in paint which has been well thinned with turpentine or white spirit. Use a light pastel colour or ordinary white. Allow this to dry for about half an hour, after which time the thinning agent will have evaporated sufficiently.

Allow yourself to be led by the materials and at first work without any preconceived ideas. The object of this exercise is to practise applying swatches of colour, one on top of the other, by means of setting the colours down on the still-wet paint layers.

Try to keep your colour as bright as possible so that no muddying results.

I Mix the required colour on the palette. Set down two groups of colours; one dark and one light. Do not thin the paint, or thin it with only a very small amount of medium, so that the brushstrokes remain visible, something which is essential in this technique.

II Wash the brush out in white spirit and dry it with a tissue. Brushes should be cleaned after each colour has been used in order to preserve the clarity and brightness of the colours. Apply to the lighter area a few strokes in a still lighter colour. Colour mixing will take place because the underlying paint is still wet.

III   Try to treat the darker area in the same way, by applying swatches of paint, one over the other. Allow the colours to mix only through the brushstroke. This means that you must consider beforehand which colour you will apply. Do not alter the brushstroke by rubbing or brushing: if you do this you lose the essence of the Alla Prima technique.

IV   If you apply a light colour, it is particularly necessary to work with a clean brush, otherwise you get an unwanted mixing of the colours. Use a different type of brush occasionally so that you experience the effects of both flat and round brushes.

V   Experiment in lightening, or toning down, areas of colour with the paint.

VI   Change the direction of the brushstroke occasionally to produce a different texture.

VII Vertical lines can give different effects than horizontal lines. Allow these lines to cross each other now and then.

VIII Handle the brush in different ways, so that you discover which method suits you best.

IX Continue to add colour until you see that the applied colour no longer produces the effect you expected.

The colours have then mixed too much. Try to discover the point at which the paint remains bright and the point at which it threatens to become muddy.

Now look again at the Alla Prima paintings illustrated in this chapter. Notice the different ways in which the brushes have been used.

I   The subject is a still life.
  The actual work of painting again begins with the arrangement: old empty wine bottles on a draped cloth. In this phase the colour, form and composition are already important; they will determine the eventual painting. The fall of light is also important. Jacqie Vink has chosen to set up her still life in front of the window, so that the light from outside falls through the glass and highlights its colours. Her easel stands approximately 2½ metres from her subject and that is why time and again she must observe and revise the subject from that distance.

II   First, a thin underpainting is applied. This is done, on the one hand, to promote a bond between the paint and the surface (material/technical), and, on the other hand, to break up the white of the canvas (preparation/concentration).
  The still life is then executed in charcoal, with the emphasis being placed on the right-hand group of bottles. However, the artist will not feel completely bound by the sketch.
  The charcoal drawing is a guideline which she will follow or, wherever she feels necessary, depart from, in order to give a different interpretation.

THE ALLA PRIMA TECHNIQUE IN PICTURES
AN ARTIST AT WORK

If you examine Paul Versteeg's painting on page 81 and that of Jacqie Vink on an Alla Prima painting, we have intentionally chosen the same subject, namely *Still Life with Bottles.*

If you examine Paul Versteeg's painting on page 81 and that of Jacqie Vink on page 95, you will see the enormous differences in technique and in the use of materials. The artist's interpretation is also completely different.

  Apart from the fact that Versteeg's picture is painted layer by layer, with an intermediate drying time between layers, and that by Jacqie Vink is executed in the wet-on-wet technique, the former is immobile and peaceful while the latter is lively and almost explosive.

III The first essential touches of colour are laid down, that is to say, the facets which most appeal to the artist at that moment.

For Jacqie Vink, these are the vertical lines of the bottles. She already captures light and dark areas. In this phase, the artist is working with well-thinned paint and using broad, stiff hog's hair brushes – she prefers to use several at the same time, so that she can continue to work without breaking off.

IV The artist is working swiftly and dynamically. The bottles and the cloth are brought together here with slashes of colour. The paint is applied less sparsely.

The artist Jacqie Vink demonstrates how she set about making an Alla Prima painting. Because she has chosen a large format canvas, 100 x 130 cm, it was not possible to complete the painting in one sitting. The second sitting, however, took place on the following day. The paint was still wet, so that she was able to continue with the wet-on-wet technique.

V The subject is now as if closed in by part of the background. Almost the entire canvas has been worked. The artist has chosen a dark background so that attention is drawn to the bottles. Now that the whole subject has been given its form, she directs herself primarily to the areas of light and dark, while at the same time keeping the composition as a whole in mind. Nowhere does she work in small areas. The paint is hardly thinned at all.

VI The artist continues to maintain her strong brush handling, even in the details. It is necessary to continually study the canvas from a distance. She is clearly guarding against the 'killing' of the colours. The brushes are thoroughly cleaned in white spirit and then washed with soft soap. The bright colours must be retained.

VII Further accents are painted in. The strongest light effects are applied in the last layers.

VIII Now is the time to pause. Then follows a critical appraisal in which every part of the painting is examined under a magnifying glass.

IX The following day the final touches are applied. Jacqie Vink named her painting *La Vie d'une Artiste.*

KNIFE TECHNIQUES

Paste-like paint, applied with a painting knife, is preferred for paintings made with the knife technique. The characteristic of a painting in this technique is the texture which is created by the use of the painting knife. Paintings of this kind are usually not detailed, but much more orientated towards colour and texture. Knife techniques can be employed in the layered, as well as in the Alla Prima technique.

DESCRIPTION OF TECHNIQUE BASED ON ACTUAL PAINTINGS

24 October Between 11.48 and 12.36 – undated K.R. SONDORBURG

The structures were applied with a straight painting knife. The Alla Prima technique was used for this painting. For the large part the white and black have mixed.

Other techniques, such as splashing and scratching, were also used. In some places, the paint has been worked with a brush and perhaps also with the fingers.

Diptych in White and Black – 1980 THEO STEVENS

This diptych was made completely with a painting knife. Only a single structure was applied. The emphasis lies on the ornamental composition and the tension between the planes.

These simple panels consist of one paint layer which was applied directly to the surfaces.

Sky near Honfleur
– 1952
NICOLAS DE STAEL

In this landscape, in which the sky forms the large part of the canvas, the knife technique shows up well. The landscape was painted in layers and the paint is laid down in regular, horizontal knife strokes. At times several paint tints were taken on the knife together and applied to the canvas. This is clearly discernable in the darker area of the sky.

Summer – undated
CONSTANT PERMEKE

The knife technique can also be combined with the brush technique, and this painting by Permeke is a good example of this. In the sky area, particularly, the painting knife is frequently used, with very thin oil paint glazing applied over. This creates the intense glow, by which he portrays the sun-drenched landscape. The brush technique is clearly perceptible in the foreground.

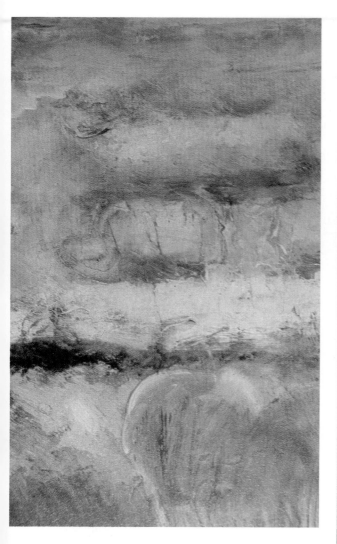

Detail: This enlargement of an area in the centre right of the painting gives a good idea of how brush and knife were used.

In this composition an underpainting in whites was first laid down with the knife. After drying, a thin paint layer in various tints of grey was applied with brush and painting knife, without completely covering the underpainting. Next, the colour planes were laid down with a brush and thinned oil paint.

A pattern of lines was applied, which was then partly painted over. More lines were applied over the last paint layer to accentuate the planes of colour.

Composition
– undated
FRANCIS BOTT

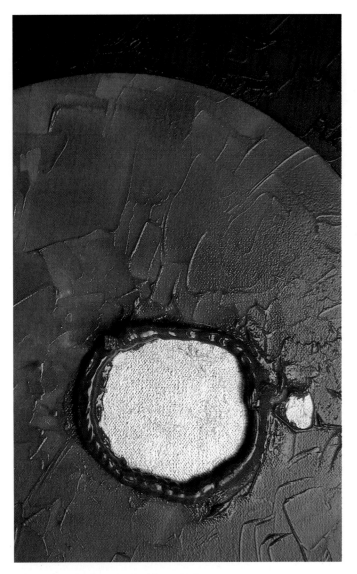

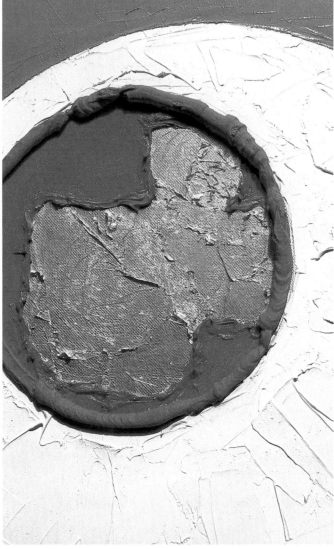

When employing the knife technique, as a rule semi-opaque or opaque sorts of paint are used. You must also stick to the painting principle of 'oily over less oily', while nevertheless working the paint in a paste-like form. If the oil paint is thinned too much, the knife structure is destroyed.

In this detail you see that transparent madder lake is used sensibly. A thin, but not thinned, layer of paint was laid down with a painting knife, while the ring of paint was applied directly from the tube. Because the thick madder lake ring does not cover a large area and could dry uniformly, the paint did not wrinkle.

Be careful with the use of transparent colours. Preferably, this sort of paint should only be worked in thin layers. Thickly applied transparent paint layers can wrinkle during drying.

In this detail from a painting you can see the use of opaque paste-like paint which has been applied with a painting knife. The paint in the raised circle was applied to the canvas directly from the tube. (The gold-coloured area consists of gold leaf.)

TRYING OUT MATERIALS:
THE KNIFE TECHNIQUE

Prepare your surfaces well and apply a sparse underpainting in order to promote a binding between the surface and the paint. Use the painting medium sparingly so that the paint remains paste-like.

Painting knives are available in many different forms. Do not purchase too many, because you can make different structures with a single knife by varying the way in which you use it.

In making your trial pieces, use the two painting knives from your basic stock of materials. If, in the long term, it turns out that you want to concern yourself more intensively with the knife technique, then you can broaden your range of knives. Do not confuse painting knives with palette knives.

I Lay down a thin layer of transparent oil paint with a pointed painting knife. Do this without thinning the paint, but scrape it thinly over the surface with the knife. Try to lay down the structure in different directions. The surface contributes towards the structure. Let the paint dry.

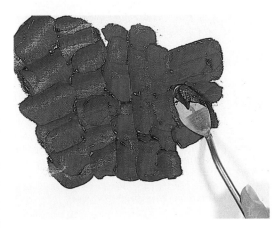

II Make a similar experiment as I. This time, however, use a rounded knife and an opaque paint. The paint will be applied thicker because of the rounded form of the knife; the knife does not make as much contact with the surface as a straight knife. The surface is now less visible. Thicker paint layers should be left to dry for a longer period so as not to run the risk of the paint being damaged by the knife when the next paint layer is applied.

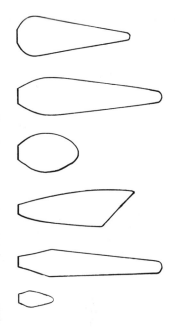

Painting knives are available in a variety of shapes. Each knife gives its own characteristic stroke.

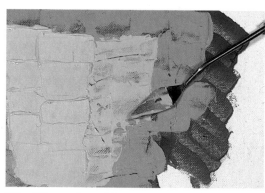

III A second layer is now applied to the first trial piece. In this instance, an opaque paint is used. The paint is worked so that the underlying layer still contributes to the whole. There is no mixing of colours because the blue layer is dry; the localized changes in colour are due to the fact that the paint is showing through the top layer. Allow this piece to dry.

IV We apply a third layer. This can be done thickly, to cover the underlying layers, or thinly, so that the underlying layers show through.

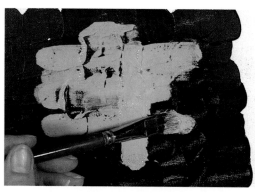

V Also make a few experiments with a painting knife, used in combination with a brush.

VI Lay down a layer of paint with a painting knife.

These experiments you have made in the layered painting technique can also be done in the Alla Prima technique. The advantage of this is that you can complete the experiments one after the other, because the layers are laid down wet, one over the other.

VII Lay down a second layer over it. The colours mix together.

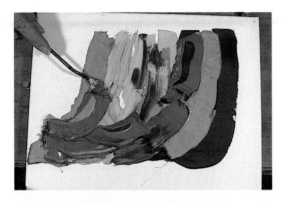

VIII When still more layers are applied, still more colours are created.

Now examine the illustrations in this chapter again. You will be better able to recognize and understand the techniques which were used in the paintings.

THE KNIFE TECHNIQUE IN PICTURES
AN ARTIST AT WORK

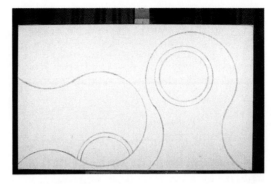

I The subject is drawn in charcoal on the white, prepared surface, after which the loose charcoal particles are brushed off with a feather (duck's wing) so that the paint will not be contaminated when it is applied.

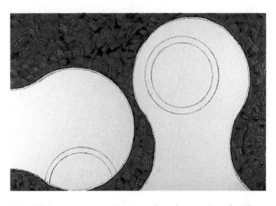

II Transparent ultramarine is used to indicate the dark depths in which the frogmen find themselves. The colour strokes follow the curved lines of the divers, so that the turbulence in the water is accentuated.

Frogmen – 1987
THEO STEVENS

Because the knife technique is a direct method of working which requires a considerable amount of skill, we have chosen a subject which is not too complicated, to enable you to follow the various steps.

Frogmen was painted on a linen surface. The artist used four different painting knives, each of which gave a different structure to the paint.

The subject is worked stylishly. It therefore contains few details, which is important when the knife technique is employed.

III The ultramarine is applied in such a way that the white surface contributes to the texture. Because this transparent paint is worked thinly, no wrinkling of the paint can take place.

IV   Because the thinned paint is spread smooth with a painting knife, the black has little structure. This layer serves as an underpainting for a second – structured – layer to be applied later.

V   The 'windows' in the frogmen's suits are painted in ochre and cadmium red.

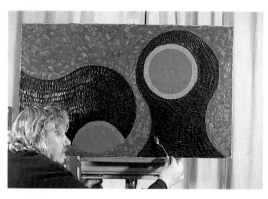

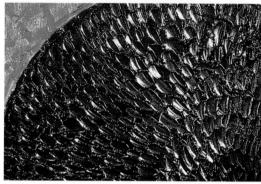

VI   The second black layer is applied, with paint that has been made a bit more oily by adding a little medium. Notice the way in which the painting knife is employed.

VII   The structure gives the frogmen the scaly appearance of fish. The touches of paint are built up rhythmically.

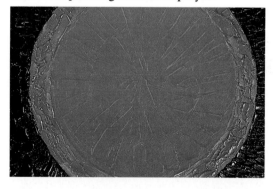

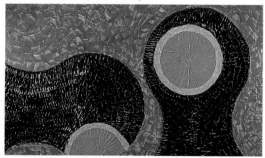

VIII   This texture was created by applying the paint with the side of the painting knife. With every application, the paint is raised.

IX   The final phase. It is clearly visible that the ultramarine, which was applied directly to the surface, has faded in places because the oil from the paint has been absorbed by the surface. After the paint has dried a little, the artist will treat this blue area with re-touching varnish.

  This problem did not occur in the black paint layers because the underlying layer already contained enough oil.

  The artist will not be able to apply a finishing varnish until after eight to 12 months – depending on the thickness of the paint – because only then will the paint be completely dry.

IMPASTO TECHNIQUES

The impasto technique is a technique in which fairly thick layers of paint are applied to the surface with a painting knife or a brush. Different painting techniques can be used to produce an impasto. It can be built up layer by layer or it can be made using the wet-on-wet technique. Once the impasto layers are dry, glazed (transparent) layers of paint can be applied over them.

To be able to lay down still thicker layers of paint without running the risk that they will wrinkle or crack, a special painting paste is mixed with the oil paint. Another possibility is first to apply a relief to the surface with a paste and then, after it has dried, work it with oil paint. Finally, filling agents can be added to the oil paint or the paste. They change or fill out the structure of the top layer.

DESCRIPTION OF TECHNIQUES BASED ON ACTUAL PAINTINGS

Woman in a Chemise – 1921
PABLO PICASSO

In this layered painting, the background is smoothly painted and the paint is applied more thickly on the body. Picasso has clearly used the impasto technique in the chemise, where the paint has the most mass.

Notre Dame Under Snow – undated
ALBERT LEBOURG

This painting was largely constructed with painting knives. The impasto technique is most strongly expressed in the foreground.

Hélène – undated
GUSTAVE MOREAU

It is hardly believable that Moreau was able to depict such a still, delicate figure using such a coarse technique as impasto.

Hélène is painted on a sheer blue background, which plays an important part in the entire picture.

Hélène herself is laid down in thickly-applied slashes of paint and radiates an almost magical effect of light. The impasto surface glistens. The artist scratched the paint in various places and, after the paint had dried, he rubbed it until it shone. Moreau painted many mythological figures and often combined watercolours and oil paints.

Rouen Cathedral
– 1894
CLAUDE MONET

The areas of light and shadow play a central role in this Impressionist painting, which was given a rough impasto surface.

Detail: This detail, the rose above the vestibule, shows us that Monet began with a rough under-painting. Over this he laid down innumerable colour tints to strengthen the impasto effect.

AUXILIARY MATERIALS FOR THE APPLICATION OF IMPASTOS

In the impasto technique, it is preferable to use semi-opaque or opaque types of paint when applying pure oil paint in fairly thick layers. When transparent paint is laid down in thick layers, it tends to wrinkle while drying and this causes the surface to ripple. However, thin, transparent layers of paint can be applied over a dry, thick paint layer. Although a thick layer of opaque oil paint wrinkles less readily than an equally thick transparent paint layer, it will also wrinkle if the layer is applied *too* thickly.

This wrinkling is the result of uneven drying. The drying of oil paint is brought about by the taking in of oxygen from the air which, at first, causes a skin to form on the surface of the paint. If the oil content of the paint layer is too high – and therefore the solid-matter content too low – the paint directly under the surface shrinks and this causes the upper layer to wrinkle. Uneven drying can also result in shrinkage cracks appearing in the paint.

To counteract wrinkles and shrinkage cracks, the paint industry has developed a special painting paste.

PAINTING PASTE   Painting paste consists of drying vegetable oils, synthetic resins and thickening agents and it is mixed with the paint to counteract shrinking and splitting of thick paint layers. The paste is transparent and colourless and has the same consistency as oil paint.

Mixing the oil paint with paste has little or no effect on the colour nor on the textures produced by the knife and the brush. A good mixing proportion is 1 : 3 (one part paint to three parts paste). The minimum proportion that may be used is 1 : 1; if less paste is added, the danger of wrinkling and cracking again arises. Painting paste is a putty-like medium which slightly lowers the degree of gloss and shortens the drying process of the paint. The greater the quantity of medium added, the shorter the drying time. Painting paste can be thinned with turpentine or white spirit if necessary.

All painting materials should be cleaned with white spirit after the use of painting paste. Carry out a few experiments with this painting paste, in one or more colours. Do this using a painting knife. The paint and paste are mixed beforehand on your palette with a palette knife. Lay down thick layers.

UNDERPAINTING WHITE Another method of precluding wrinkles and cracks in the oil paint is to first lay down an underpainting in relief, over which the actual oil painting is made, so that the paint layers are of the thickness required. *Underpainting white*, a special sort of paint, is used for this purpose. It is a very pasty type of oil paint which consists of drying vegetable oils, resins and titanium white. It can be laid down in several thick layers and dries fairly quickly – one or two days – depending on the thickness. When it is dry, the oil painting can be applied over it. Underpainting white is applied to the surface from the palette with a painting knife or brush. The texture of the knife or brush remains visible. Underpainting white can be thinned with white spirit or turpentine. Painting materials should be cleaned with white spirit after underpainting white has been used. If a tinted underpainting is required, a little oil paint can be mixed with the underpainting white. This gives a pastel shade. Mix on your palette and apply the paint with a painting knife or brush. Use a stiff brush for the experiments with underpainting white. Carry out the test by using the underpainting both pure and mixed with oil paint.

The differences between painting paste and underpainting white are now clear: painting paste is a putty-like medium which is added to the oil paint to counteract wrinkling and cracking of the paint; underpainting white is applied to the surface in structured layers and after drying can be painted over.

Painting paste is transparent and can be mixed with oil paint without influencing the colour.

Underpainting white is a paste-like type of oil paint. Pastel tints are created when it is mixed with colour.

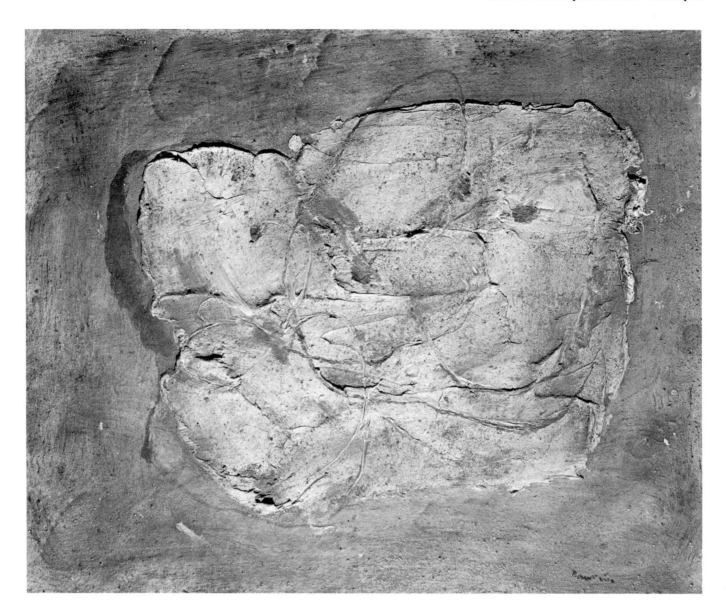

Fruit – 1943
JEAN FAUTRIER

This is a clear example of how a relief applied in underpainting white is employed. The knife strokes are easily visible. A glazed layer of paint is applied over the relief. Moreover, a few extra areas enhance the plastic effect of the underpainting.

EXPERIMENTS WITH UNDERPAINTING
WHITE   Instead of carrying out a series
of experiments on different surfaces,
here you can experiment by employing
different techniques, one over the other,
on a single surface.

II   Enclose the structure, so that it is left blank, as it were. In this way transparent as well as opaque areas can be created in an impasto painting.

I   Lay down a structure in underpainting
white with a stiff brush and allow it to dry.
Then apply a thinned layer of oil paint. The
brushstroke in the Underpainting white remains visible.

III   Apply touches of colour over the impasto layer. Now the brushstrokes of the newly applied layer dominate. The structure of the brushstrokes in the underpainting white is lost, but the material still contributes to the density of the impasto.

MODELLING PASTE   Modelling paste is used if large, thick layers of relief are required for the underpainting of an impasto.

We have not yet added modelling paste to our basic stock of materials, but it can always be purchased, if necessary. We have included the use of modelling paste in this chapter, because it is often used in the making of an impasto.

Modelling paste is thick, water-containing, filler-like paste which consists of white, pigmented synthetic dispersions and thickening agents. This paste is usually applied to the surface with a painting knife. A hard surface is therefore the most suitable; flexible surfaces can be distorted by the heavy paste layers. The surface must be oil-free in order to promote a good binding between it and the modelling paste. The paste dries in a few minutes or some hours, depending on the thickness of the layers. The paste can be painted over.

IV   The Alla Prima technique can also be applied by laying down touches of wet paint over each other. Because the underpainting white has provided a layer of relief, it appears that the layer of oil paint is thicker than it actually is. Because it is, in fact, thin, it will not crack or wrinkle.

V   Because the paint has been somewhat spread, the texture of the underpainting is again visible. Now allow the trial piece to dry for some time.

VI   Here, the surface of the dry trial piece is scrubbed with a little unthinned white paint. Through this, the texture of the paint layers and some texture of the underpainting are again visible.

EXPERIMENTS WITH MODELLING PASTE   In contrast to underpainting white, modelling paste is not an oil paint, but despite this it is perfectly satisfactory for setting down layers of relief in the underpainting. Different techniques can again be used to execute an oil painting over these layers.

Modelling paste is also used to fix objects to the surface before they are completely or partially painted over. This method of working is often employed when working with non-paint-related materials.

Used painting materials must be immediately cleaned in water, so that the synthetic material in the paste does not harden.

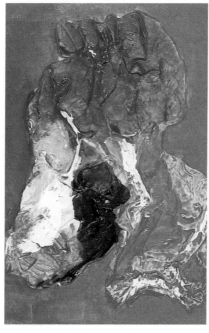

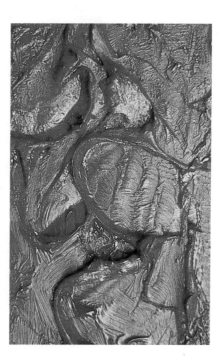

I A sparse overpainting in oil paint is laid down over a structure of modelling paste.

II The oil paint is then applied less thinned. In this way you can apply more or fewer opaque paint layers, while the underpainting provides the structure.

III Another possibility is to thinly apply transparent paint over such a structured underpainting. The white underlayer then shows through the paint layer and so contributes to the plastic effect.

Working with non-paint-related materials will be extensively discussed in one of the volumes in this series, *Mixed Techniques.*

The following experiments are intended to inform, and to clarify and complete the possibilities of using modelling paste.

III The modelling paste is laid down with a painting knife in order to obtain a greater relief effect and to bind some of the objects together. A single shape is used only as additional filling material; to achieve a certain depth, others will be included in the design.

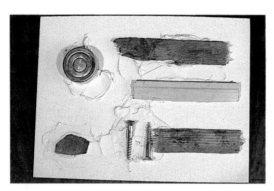

I This is an example of the handling of arbitrary objects fixed with modelling paste.

IV Because the modelling paste was applied very thickly, it must be left to dry for three days, after which time the paste is very hard. Layers of oil paint can now be applied.

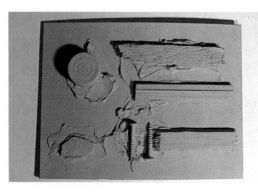

II After the paste has dried, a coloured underlayer is applied in oil paint.

V The objects can be completely absorbed into the paint layers or remain unpainted if this is an advantage in the composition and the expression of the material.

The foregoing demonstrates that there are many methods of producing work in the impasto technique, ranging from the use of pure paint to the employment of thickening and filling agents.

Whichever impasto technique you employ, always be guided by the technical limitations of the different materials and always employ the painting principle of oily over less oily ('fat over lean').

Do not only stick to experiments to achieve the various effects. Primarily it is about painting itself, as a serious well-thought out and lived-through experience in which a particular auxiliary material can certainly be employed.

AN IMPASTO TECHNIQUE IN PICTURES:
A CLOSER LOOK AT DETAILS OF A PAINTING

I   This painting is executed in an impasto technique. It is painted in whites and earth colours such as yellow, ochre, sienna, umber and black. It was made after the demolition of the painter's home. Though the house has disappeared, its impression remains visible, a silent witness, as it were, on the wall of the house next door.

The open, blackened chimney flue is the darkest part of the painting and therefore attracts the attention. You can clearly see where the floors once were, while on the left of the painting traces of the staircases which led to these floors are still visible.

II   An underpainting in underpainting white was applied to the impregnated surface during which the canvas was left blank in some places. This underpainting was laid down with Gussows. By mixing the underpainting white with a small amount of oil paint, different white tints were created.

This painting, *The Demolition*, is a good example of how auxiliary materials, used in a well-thought out way, can be applied to impasto techniques, because they contribute to the impression the artist had in mind.

III Later, these different whites were partly given glazes for which earth colours, thinned with medium, were used, In this detail it can be clearly seen that the thickness of the paint layers differs greatly. The linen structure of the canvas is partly visible.

IV In part of the oil paint, finely ground cinders were worked in as filling material with which the cement and lime remnants of the plaster work are indicated. This created the rough structure which is so characteristic of old walls.

V In the detail of part of the chimney flue, thick and thin layers of paint lie next to each other, which heightens the plastic effect. The thick brown paint layers were in part directly applied to the canvas from the tube. In other places the paint, mixed with transparent painting paste, was applied to the canvas with a painting knife.

VI The use of a painting knife is also clearly visible here. On one hand, the paint has been scraped away which made furrows in the paint layer, on the other hand there are areas of paint which have become thicker.

VII Different painting techniques were used in making this painting. The artist allowed the underpainting to dry after the first application. Then wet layers were carefully laid down, one over the other, without these layers mixing, however. After a further drying, the painting was given very thin, transparent layers of paint.